Merry Christmas to Jeremiah
From: Grandpa Fellows
Dec. 25, 1986

DINOSAURS

Author
David Lambert

Advisory Consultant
Barry Cox M.A., Ph.D., D.Sc.

Editor
Jennifer Justice

This 1982 edition is published by Bonanza Books, distributed by Crown Publishers, Inc.

Originally published in Great Britain by Grisewood & Dempsey Limited

Printed in Italy by Vallardi Industrie Grafiche, Milan
Color separations by Newsele Litho, Milan.

Library of Congress Cataloging in Publication Data
Lambert, David, 1932-
  Dinosaurs.

  Originally published: New York : Crown
Publishers, 1978.
  1. Dinosaurs.   I. Title.
[QE862.D5L42 1982]   568.9'1   82-4502
ISBN 0-517-38320-9   AACR2

h g f e d c b

DINOSAURS

DAVID LAMBERT

Bonanza Books · New York

Contents

Giants of the Past 6

The Fossil Hunters 8

Life Begins 14

The First Dinosaurs 24

Gentle Giants 32

Fearful Fangs 40

Bird-hipped Bipeds 50

Armoured Animals 60

Adventurers in Air and Water 68

Vanishing Dinosaurs 78

The Search Today 84

Glossary 90

Index and Acknowledgements 94

About This Book

Ever since scientists first realized that out-sized fossil bones belonged to a hitherto unknown group of creatures long vanished from the earth, dinosaurs have proved an endless source of fascination to people of all ages. The world the dinosaurs inhabited was a strange one, yet the animals played out roles astonishingly similar to those we observe today among predators and prey.

Dinosaurs leads the reader into these remarkable scenes from the past, beginning with an introduction to the world the dinosaurs inherited. It covers the three great periods of Mesozoic time, from 225 to 65 million years ago, and the varied groups of dinosaurs that emerged: the voracious flesh-eaters; the huge, lumbering plant-eaters; heavily armoured beasts; and the 'duck-billed' dinosaurs, with their curious range of head crests. Many of the creatures that shared the dinosaurs' world are also described and illustrated, including the first mammals and the winged reptiles that ruled the skies.

Finally, the book probes the fascinating mystery that still puzzles the experts: why, after 140 million years of domination, the dinosaurs died out – not as individual species, but as a complete group. The closing chapter examines the work that is going on today – both in the field and in the museum – in an attempt to shed new light on some of the most remarkable creatures that ever lived.

Giants of the Past

A herd of Apatosaurus stops at a
waterhole in the mist of a Jurassic
morning. These massive dinosaurs,
each of which weighed more than
five elephants, were among the
largest animals ever to have lived
on earth.

About 200 years ago people began to take an interest in huge fossil bones locked in the stone of cliffs, mines and quarries.

Bit by bit, palaeontologists (scientists who study fossils) pieced these bone puzzles together. They were able to assemble vertebrae, ribs and skulls to make single, individual animals. Using wires, clamps and other aids, these explorers into the past rebuilt whole skeletons. With only bare bones before them, anatomists were able to work out the sizes and shapes of the muscles which had been anchored to the bones. They then guessed intelligently at the creatures' other long-vanished characteristics – especially skin texture and colour. Unfamiliarity, of course, led to errors. One leading American palaeontologist located a skull at the tip of a tail; a British expert placed a spiked thumb on a nose.

As the 19th century advanced, frenzied digging by rival American teams revealed still bigger bones by the crate load. There was now no doubt that long ago had lived a whole zoo of monsters of more terrible aspect than the worst ogres in any fairy tale. Such were many of the beasts we call dinosaurs.

By the middle of the 20th century, scientists the world over had a rich tally of dinosaur fossils from various continents. They had deduced that dinosaurs were slow-witted, sluggish, cold-blooded reptiles of outlandish size that had dominated life on land from 205 million to about 65 million years ago, when they mysteriously died out.

Today, many of the long-cherished notions about dinosaurs are being questioned. Experts – chiefly American – have challenged accepted ideas about how these animals' massive bodies worked. They hold that dino-saurs were, in fact, active, warm-blooded beasts, very different from their reptile ancestors. Moreover, they argue, many dinosaurs were relatively big-brained and were at least as intelligent as the ostrich that some of these beasts so closely resembled.

Another theory takes this idea further. Living birds, it argues, are direct descendants of one dinosaur group. Birds, in fact, are dinosaurs – the sole, successful, survivors of a line otherwise cut off 60 million years before Man's first recognizable ancestors put in an appearance.

Controversy still rages about precisely what dinosaurs were and looked like, how they behaved, and how their bodies worked. But even as the dust of academic conflict continues to whirl we can paint a picture of the dinosaur world which most palaeontologists working today would accept.

The Fossil Hunters

The first dinosaur fossils were discovered by accident – it was to be many years before the great beasts we know about today were reconstructed from these fragments of bone and teeth.

Everything we know about the dinosaurs we owe to their remains preserved as fossils in the rocks. Greek scholars were finding and describing fossil seashells more than 2400 years ago. But the mystery of what fossils really were and how they got there has been unravelled only in the last three centuries.

Some people believed that the devil had lodged fossils in the rocks to puzzle mankind. Another notion was that a strange power in the earth had made fossils in the forms of living things, but failed to give them life.

By the 18th century most people knew that fossil seashells had once been parts of animals that lived beneath the sea. But how had these shells become embedded in the rocks on land – even high up among the mountains?

The Great Flood

The usual answer was that they were stranded by a great flood that (so the Bible said) had been God's punishment for Man's misdeeds. Only by about two centuries ago did people grasp that many of the rocks beneath our feet had once been mud or sand upon the sea floor; that these sediments had been squashed and hardened into rock; and that heaving of the restless earth had raised the rock above the waves with the fossils in it. We now know, too, that land animals, including dinosaurs, sometimes fell into a river, lake or sea, to become embedded in its floor. In time the rocks with their remains were also lifted above water. Wind, sun, frost and running water often wore away the rocky covering and left the fossil dinosaurs exposed. Of the millions of dinosaurs that must have died, a mere handful probably became fossilized.

Chance plays a large part in determining when and where a fossil forms. Fossils can occur in one of several ways. Usually a creature's soft parts soon rot away. But bones and teeth last longer. Water seeping down through the rocks may deposit minerals in pores

Fossils are formed under special conditions which enable them to withstand millions of years of entombment within the earth. When a dinosaur, such as this hadrosaur, dies, its body may settle under water.

More and more layers of sediment pile upon the skeleton, compressing the deeper layers so that they are gradually turned into rock. Later, earth movements uplift the land, exposing the rocks.

within the bones. In time, calcite, silica or iron pyrites will harden the bones and strengthen them against the crushing pressures of the rocks above. Sometimes minerals replace a bone or even an entire skeleton, turning it to stone. Such petrified bones may still keep the shapes of the original bones.

Sometimes water seeping through porous rock dissolves away the bones of creatures embedded in the rock. A hollow is left, preserving the outline of the vanished object. Fossils of this kind are known as *moulds*.

Fossils may also be preserved in amber, peat, tar and ice. But dinosaur fossils are all found in rock.

Early Discoveries

By the 1800s people knew that many fossils represented creatures unlike any still alive. Keen fossil hunters began collecting specimens. In 1810 Mary Anning had prised a complete ichthyosaur fossil from sea cliffs at Lyme Regis, in southern England.

The flesh and soft parts of the animal soon decay, but its bones and teeth remain in their original position. Soon, a layer of fine mud and sand will sift across the skeleton, gently encasing it. In time, minerals replace the bone.

The rocks are now slowly eroded away by the weathering of wind and rain. Finally, the fossil relic of a creature dead for tens of millions of years becomes exposed again at the earth's surface.

Opposite page: Huge fossil relics of the dinosaurs embedded in rock. Some of the early discoverers of such remains believed that they were all that was left of animals drowned in the Biblical Flood.

She was 11 years old at the time. Mary went on to become the first person to make a living by discovering and selling fossils. The rocks that Mary Anning probed date from the Age of Dinosaurs. But the discovery of the dinosaurs themselves came farther east in England.

The man responsible was Gideon Mantell, a country doctor with a life-long passion for collecting fossils. Tradition has it that one spring day in 1822 Dr Mantell set off to visit a patient. His wife went with him for the ride. While their horse and carriage waited at the patient's home, Mrs Mantell wandered down the road. She noticed a pile of stones put there for filling ruts. In these stones she glimpsed fossil teeth.

Dr Mantell had never seen such teeth before. Intrigued, he found the quarry where the stones had come from, and discovered more teeth. Mantell knew these fossils were extremely old because the rocks they belonged to were Cretaceous. He showed several famous scientists the teeth. None believed them to be

ancient, or anything but those of a mammal or perhaps a fish.

Mantell remained stubbornly sure that he had stumbled onto some unknown type of ancient animal. He discovered that the teeth were like an iguana's, but far larger. In 1825 he named their long-dead owner *Iguanodon* ('iguana tooth'). Seven years later a mass of *Iguanodon* teeth and bones turned up in a different quarry. No one now doubted that *Iguanodon* had lived. Meanwhile, huge bones of a *Megalosaurus* had been dug up farther away, in Oxfordshire.

By 1841 enough such fossils had been found to convince the leading British anatomist Richard Owen that there had once lived a whole prehistoric tribe of huge, lizard-like reptiles. He named them 'dinosaurs' from the Greek words *deinos* and *sauros*, translated by him as 'fearfully great lizards'.

By 1854 Owen had had the sculptor Waterhouse Hawkins recreate a whole zoo of lifesize concrete dinosaurs. Workmen stood them among

Opposite page: An early effort at visualizing prehistoric beasts. Waterhouse Hawkins' Crystal Palace studio in 1853 contained his models of a mammal (far left), reptile (near right), amphibian (near left) and two dinosaurs. These were Iguanodon (centre) and Hylaeosaurus or 'Wealden Lizard' (far right). Iguanodon's stance and nose horn were two of many errors.

Othniel Charles Marsh (1831–1899) proved North America's most prolific discoverer of dinosaurs. His greatest triumphs included excavations at Como Bluff, Wyoming, seen below in a contemporary watercolour sketch. There lay an 11-km (7-mile) long cemetery of gigantic sauropod and other bones.

Above: Muscle power applied to block and tackle helped this team to lift the colossal load of a Diplodocus's petrified thigh bone. Similar methods salvaged many such monster finds from Utah's Dinosaur Quarry in the early part of this century.

Edward Drinker Cope (1840–1897) (right) and Othniel Marsh (below right) were the chief discoverers of fossil dinosaurs in North America. Cope wrote his first scientific study at the age of six. In 1876 his Montana expedition found traces of 20 dinosaur species.

the trees and lakes of south London's Sydenham Park, near the famous Crystal Palace exhibition hall. They still stand, somewhat the worse for wear and largely discredited by modern knowledge of the animals' true shapes and postures. But they are nonetheless imposing to look at.

American Discoveries

As the 19th century wore on, people unearthed more dinosaurs in Britain and on the European continent. But soon North America began to yield the most exciting finds for 'big-game' fossil hunters.

Americans had actually been discovering the fossil bones and footprints of dinosaurs before the English found *Iguanodon*, but they did not know it. In 1800 Pliny Moody saw huge fossil footprints in the Connecticut Valley. Their bird-like shape led some observers to believe that they were the footprints of the raven sent by Noah from the Ark to search out dry land. No one dreamt that the tracks, pressed deep into what had once been mudflats, were those of a Triassic dinosaur.

The year after Hawkins' Crystal Palace monsters were finished marked the real start of America's dinosaur discoveries. In 1855, sent west with a government mapping expedition, the young geologist Ferdinand Hayden found fossil teeth in the wild badlands of Montana. In 1858 the anatomist Joseph Leidy identified some as those of a plant-eating dinosaur he named *Trachodon* ('rugged tooth'). Today we know this as the duck-billed dinosaur *Anatosaurus*. Leidy identified other teeth as those of a ferocious megalosaur that he christened *Deinodon horridus* ('most horrible of the terror teeth').

But the climax of American dinosaur hunting began in March 1877. Two schoolmasters – Arthur Lakes and O. W. Lucas – separately stumbled on colossal fossil bones projecting from the rocks in different parts of Colorado. Lakes revealed the sources of his discoveries to the well-known palaeontologist Othniel Marsh. Lucas showed his finds to Marsh's bitter rival, Edward Cope.

Soon, teams hired by these jealous scientists were prising the fossil bones of huge Jurassic creatures from their rocky tombs. The rival teams spied on each other. At least once they clashed in a free-for-all. Meanwhile they had to keep a constant watch for hostile Indians.

Both groups made dazzling discoveries that revolutionized Man's knowledge of life in Mesozoic times. All told, Cope named 9 new genera of dinosaurs; but Marsh easily surpassed this score. His tally was 19.

By 1900 the great pioneering age of dinosaur discoveries was over; but there were plenty more to come. This century, fossil hunts in lands as far apart as Tanzania and Mongolia have hugely enlarged our knowledge of this zoo of prehistoric monsters, and proved that dinosaurs had a world-wide distribution.

Hammer and chisel bare the fossil backbone of a giant from the rocky matrix that has hidden and preserved it for more than 60 million years. This fossil Tarbosaurus, an immense flesh-eater, was discovered in 1971 by a joint Polish-Mongolian team working in east-central Asia.

Life Begins

From the first speck of life came fish, amphibians and the reptile forebears of the dinosaurs. These evolutionary changes took 3000 million years.

The first dinosaurs appeared some 200 million years ago. But to trace the path that led to their arrival we must go much farther back.

Scientists have made this journey by studying sedimentary rocks. These are the rocks formed from layers of soft mud and silt deposited in seas and lakes. New layers of sediment were deposited over the old. In time the lower layers of sediment became compressed and hardened. Cliffs sometimes reveal a whole layer-cake of rocks of different ages, with the oldest at the bottom and the most recent at the top.

Each layer of sedimentary rock may hold the remains of plants and animals that lived and died when that layer was laid down. By studying successive rock layers, geologists have found that life began with tiny, simple forms that gave rise to larger, more complex plants and animals. Many species in time died out, but some produced new forms, often better suited than the old to new conditions, such as a warming or cooling climate.

Ages of the Earth
Scientists have split the long story of the earth's living things into separate 'volumes' called *eras*. Most recent are the Palaeozoic Era ('Age of Ancient Life'); Mesozoic Era ('Age of Middle Life'); and Cenozoic Era ('Age of Recent Life'). Geologists divide each of these eras into 'chapters' called *periods*, some of which they break down into smaller units known as *epochs*.

The trail leading to the dinosaurs begins with Precambrian time – a vast, misty gap some 4000 million years wide. It covers the earth's history from its birth to the Cam-

Right: The history of life on earth from Palaeozoic times to the present. Compared to Man's lifetime on earth, the dinosaurs' rule was a remarkably long one.

CAMBRIAN Marine invertebrates and algae abundant. No land plants or animals.

ORDOVICIAN Earliest marine vertebrates.

SILURIAN Jawless fishes common. First jawed fishes. First land plants.

DEVONIAN Age of Fishes. Amphibians evolve and move on to land. Earliest seed plants.

CARBONIFEROUS Amphibians spread; first reptiles. First insects. Coal forests – giant clubmosses, ferns and horsetails; first conifers.

PERMIAN Spread of reptiles; trilobites become extinct. Giant clubmosses and horsetails disappear; small seed ferns and conifers increase.

TRIASSIC First dinosaurs; evolution of herbivore and carnivore forms.

JURASSIC Dinosaurs abundant. Carnosaurs hunt huge sauropods and plated herbivores.

CRETACEOUS Dinosaurs dominate land at first. Large carnosaurs such as *Tyrannosaurus* hunt armoured, horned and duck-billed dinosaurs. But no dinosaurs outlive this period.

TERTIARY Mammals evolve rapidly. Early horses and elephant; early apes. *Australopithecus*, early 'ape-man', appears towards end of period. Increase in flowering plants. Grasses appear and spread.

QUATERNARY *Homo erectus* eventually gives rise to modern man. Woolly mammoths and rhinoceroses cope with arctic conditions. Arctic floras develop.

million years ago 4600+ 600 500 440 395 345

Cambrian Ordovician Silurian Devonian Car

Cycads and bennettitaleans appear; conifers continue widespread.

Ammonites flourish in sea.

Ammonites continue widespread; new forms of coral and sea urchins appear.

Ammonites and many other sea creatures become extinct.

trilobite *gastropod mollusc* *bivalve mollusc* *goniatite* *Cooksonia* *clubmoss* *fern* *spider* *giant horsetail* *giant clubmoss* *mayfly* *conifer* *seed fern* *ammonite* *grasshopper* *earwig* *caddis fly* *termite* *Jamoytius* *Dinichthys* *Hylo* *Ichthyostega* *Coelophysis* *Stegosaurus* *Diplodocus* *Tyrannosaurus* *Triceratops*

30   225   200   135   65   1.8   Present

| Permian | Triassic | Jurassic | Cretaceous | Tertiary | Quaternary |

Dimetrodon

Megazostrodon

Kuehneosaurus

Eryops

Rutiodon

Archaeopteryx

Pteranodon

Ichthyosaurus

Archelon

ape

Phororhacos

Australopithecus

sperm whale

mammoth

Ichthyornis

Eohippus

bennettitalean

fern

cycad

Cycads, ginkgoes common.

ginkgo

conifer

chin

First flowering plants.

Murex

bee

oak

poplar

octopus

butterfly

cherry

Above: Plant-like sponges form the setting for this Cambrian seabed scene of 600 million years ago. In the foreground are a crustacean and a number of trilobites; the segmented discs are a type of echinoderm. A shoal of jellyfish drifts by like small parachutes. No backboned animals have yet appeared on earth.

Left: Paradoxides, a giant fossil trilobite, lived in Cambrian times where Newfoundland now lies. The creature may have been a scavenger, ploughing through the mud on the sea floor in search of food. Smaller trilobites probably swam and filtered food from the surrounding water. If danger threatened, some species rolled up in a ball much like a woodlouse.

brian Period that launched the Palaeozoic Era: the first era to produce a wide variety of complex living things. The Palaeozoic Era was followed by the Mesozoic Era in which the dinosaurs themselves evolved, diversified and vanished.

Scientists now think that about 4600 million years ago the earth took shape from a whirling mass of dust. The immense heat produced as our planet formed melted the elements that make up the earth. At first the earth was a ball of molten rock, its atmosphere composed of steam and hot, poisonous gases. As the earth cooled down, its surface hardened into a solid, rocky skin whose hollows filled with seas as cooling water vapour yielded untold centuries of heavy rain.

Life remained unborn. Gradually, however, the raw materials for life were brought together. Energy from the sun's ultra-violet light playing on the atmosphere rearranged the atoms in some simple substances, forming sugars and amino acids that the rain washed into the seas. There, amino acids linked up, building proteins. In time special, complex molecules called nucleic acids appeared, each of which had the ability to grow and reproduce by dividing into two identical molecules. This property is the unique character of all living things. From such microscopic life forms came larger ones: jelly-like blobs, each built of strings of nucleic acid molecules surrounded by a protective protein-and-water coat.

These tiny organisms fed on proteins in the sea around them. Then oxygen accumulating in the atmosphere began to shut out ultra-violet light, the source of energy that had helped to produce protein foods.

Billions of living cells just starved to death. But some cells evolved the ability to harness the energy in sunlight to manufacture food from simple, handy chemicals – the process called photosynthesis. These cells were the first green plants, among them tiny blue-green algae that lived 3200 million years ago. By producing oxygen as waste, plants gradually created the right environment for animals – organisms that eat plants or one another. About half the earth's history had passed before the first animals appeared in the seas.

Each early plant and animal consisted of no more than a single cell. But, as Precambrian time went by, some cells stayed stuck together when they split, thus forging larger organisms. Eventually there appeared organisms built of different kinds of cell, each performing a specific task such as moving, feeding or reproducing. Even today, all but the lowliest life forms are based on this ancient but effective pattern.

Life in Ancient Seas

Through the Cambrian, Ordovician, and Silurian periods – the first 200 million years or so of Palaeozoic time – almost all life remained beneath the seas.

By Cambrian time seaweeds and most of the main groups of invertebrate (backboneless) animals had appeared. Among these were not only soft-bodied jellyfish and worms, but trilobites and brachiopods, which produced lime to build shells for bodily support or protection.

Plant-like corals, molluscs, and ancient relatives of squid and octopus thrived beneath Ordovician waters. And eventually some now long-lost relative of today's starfish

Above: A fossil Cephalaspis, a late Silurian jawless fish.

Below: A Silurian seabed scene of over 400 million years ago. 'Sea scorpions', some of which were up to two metres (six feet) long, and a primitive fish skulk on the bottom.

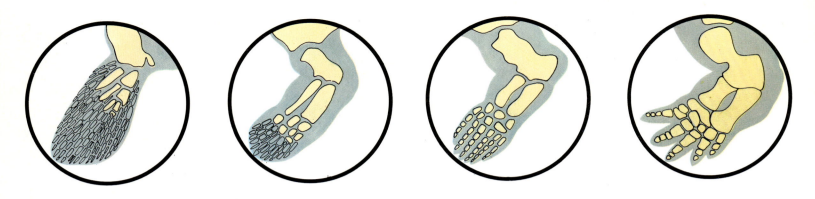

Above: Four stages by which limbs probably evolved from fins. Left: A rhipidistian fish's fin. Right: The limb of an early amphibian. The basic structure remains the same, but the bone sizes alter.

Below: A Devonian scene shows how backboned animals may have won a hold upon dry land. Pursuit by predators may have forced young, agile rhipidistians to pull themselves ashore on stumpy fins. From such pioneers came the early amphibian Ichthyostega (right).

gave rise to small, fish-like beasts; the first-known animals to manufacture bone.

This was a gigantic step forward. An internal bony skeleton can support a body and protect its vital organs, leaving its owner freer to move around than does the armour of many invertebrates. Moreover, unlike a crab, a fish can grow continuously without having to moult, or shed its shell, and thus its bodily protection. With the arrival of internal skeletons, evolution took a great stride along the path that wound from life's first, microscopically tiny building blocks towards

the biggest beasts that ever lived on land.

Colonizing the Land

The move ashore of certain backboned animals was the great evolutionary highlight of the Devonian Period (about 395 to 345 million years ago). Much had to happen, though, before this move became a possibility. First, plants had to colonize the land, since all animals depend for food on plants at first or second hand. The soft, rootless, aquatic seaweeds could never cope with dry air or the tug of gravity on land. But by 400 million years ago a

relative of the seaweeds had evolved a stiffened stem; hair-like 'roots'; internal tubes to suck up nourishment and water; and a waterproof 'skin' to stop its moist insides from drying out.

The first land plants hugged the damp shores of rivers, lakes and seas. Here, too, aquatic animals secured a beach-head. The first were ancient relatives of modern millipedes, scorpions, woodlice and other arthropod ('jointed-leg') creatures.

Many such waterside dwellers became prey to be gobbled up by the first backboned animals that ventured ashore. These vertebrates were rhipidistians, a group of lobe-finned fishes that is now extinct. Lobe-fins took their name from the long, muscular, lobe-shaped fins which some used to pull themselves

Right: Mudskippers are small, pop-eyed fish that gulp air and chase prey on wet mud at low tide. They give us a clue as to how the first fishes crawled up on land.

out of the water and on to the shore. Unlike modern fishes, lobe-fins had lungs. But they were nonetheless fishes and not designed to spend long periods out of the water.

By late Devonian times, the lobed fins of some rhipidistians had evolved into legs with five-toed feet. The long-tailed, sprawling, salamander-like owners of these limbs were amphibians – a brand-new kind of animal, at home on land as well as in the water. Now, for the first time, there were beasts whose basic skeletal design foreshadowed that of dinosaurs. But it was still a far cry from these Palaeozoic swampland sprawlers to the towering masters of the Mesozoic world.

Reptiles in the Making

The rise of the dinosaurs' reptilian ancestors occurred during the 65 million years of the Carboniferous Period – so named from the vast seams of coal (carbon) produced from the rotted and highly compressed remains of plants that lived throughout this time.

These plants formed forests clothing much of what is now eastern North America and Europe. The hot, wet, coal forests, lying just above sea level, resembled some of the dense, lush forests of the modern tropics. But their plants were very different. Giant relatives of lowly modern clubmosses towered skywards with trunks like church pil-

Above: The damp, leafy world of the Carboniferous coal forest must have been very like this modern tropical forest, with its lush, tangled foliage and steamy atmosphere.

Below: Fossils of two coal forest plants. Left, part of a giant horsetail; right, the elaborately patterned trunk of a giant clubmoss.

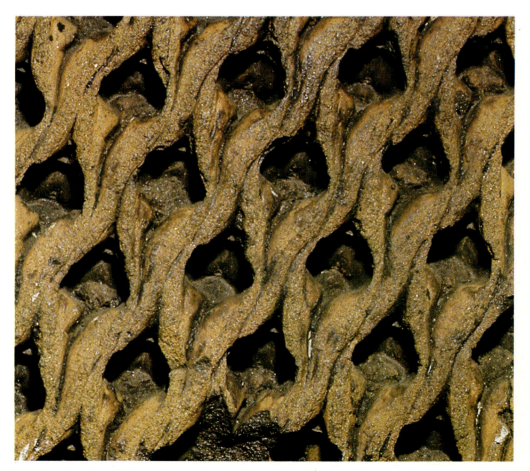

lars. Some threw out branches from the top; others bore a bushy head of leaves that sprang directly from the trunk.

There were also huge, hollow-stemmed versions of the hip-high horsetails found today in boggy pastures. Ferns – many higher than a house – helped to blot bright sunlight from the forest floor, where rotting stems and leaves yielded food for myriads of small insects and other invertebrates. From the swampy waters, strange creatures crawled up stems, split open and emerged as giant dragonflies. Grounded arthropods like millipedes and cockroaches provided food for the amphibians, while small winged insects flitted through the trees, safely out of reach of these hungry predators' jaws.

Amphibians became astonishingly plentiful and varied in the swampy forests, for as yet they had few natural enemies. The two main types of amphibian were labyrinthodonts and lepospondyls. Limbless lepospondyls swam like eels and may have lived entirely in the water. But the lepospondyls known as microsaurs had legs and may have given rise to present-day salamanders, frogs, and toads. The lepospondyls, though, did not survive the Palaeozoic Era.

Meanwhile they shared their pools with labyrinthodonts. These amphibians take their name from their

In Carboniferous times, swampy pools held lepospondyl amphibians such as the eel-like Phlegethontia, and labyrinthodonts such as the heavier-bodied Eogyrinus. From amphibians came the primitive, low-slung reptile Hylonomus in the foreground. Backboned land animals and amphibians largely ate small insects, but probably stayed away from Arthropleura, a man-length 'millipede'.

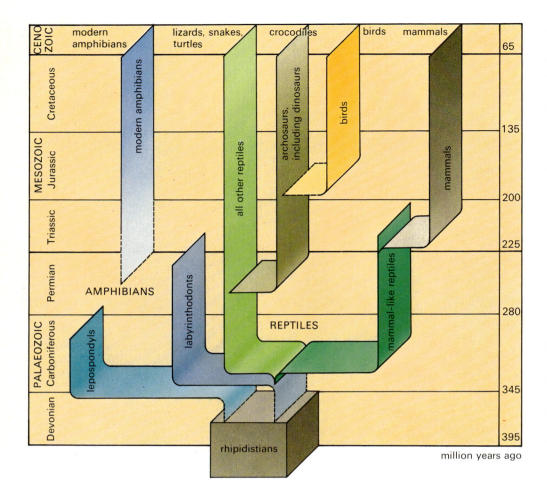

		modern amphibians		lizards, snakes, turtles	crocodiles	birds	mammals		65

Above: A simplified 'family tree' of
the reptiles and amphibians,
showing the evolution of the dinosaurs in relation to the other groups.

conical teeth, built up of labyrin-
thine structures on the same plan as
those of the lobe-finned fishes from
which they came. Some were tiny;
others grew as large as crocodiles.
Some evolved a skeleton too weak
to prop them up on land, and remained aquatic creatures. Others
evolved powerful leg muscles attached to sturdy limb bones. These
amphibians also had ear drums,
tear glands and valved nostrils,
devices that helped them to hear and
see in dry air and avoid drowning
when under water. From labyrinthodonts like these evolved the
reptiles.

Life in the Open Air

Amphibians won no more than a toe-
hold on the moist edges of the land.
Reptiles were the first truly land-
based backboned animals, and the
first to probe the dry uplands
between the river valleys. In this
adventure, the reptiles' body design
and breeding methods gave them an
enormous advantage over their amphibian relatives.

Amphibians tend to have moist,
soft skins. They soon dry up and die
if exposed to warm, dry air. Reptiles, on the other hand, protect
their moist internal organs with a
waterproof outer barrier of thick,
dry scales. Then, too, reptiles underwent changes in the bones of their
hips and feet that enabled them to
run. They were not restricted to the
wriggling walk of a salamander.
For bursts of such activity, reptiles
could also draw upon a more effective breathing system and blood
supply than those that the amphibians possessed.

Their method of reproduction
further freed reptiles from depen-
dence upon water. Most male am-

The Permian pelycosaur Dimetrodon lived in Texas. It was a
sharp-toothed predator with a skin
'sail' on its back – in reality a
radiator that helped it gain and
lose heat.

The carnivorous mammal-like reptile Lycaenops attacks a herbivorous dicynodont. These mammal-like reptiles acted out the same roles of predators and prey that lions and zebras do today.

phibians scatter sperms haphazardly under water on eggs newly laid by the females. But male reptiles fertilize eggs while they are still protected inside the females' bodies. Amphibians' eggs, encased in blobs of jelly, dry up if laid on land. Reptiles' eggs, whether leathery or hard-shelled, carry protective outer linings that keep them moist even when deposited in desert sands.

Thus, as the climate grew drier and deserts replaced the swamp forests in the Permian Period, which ended the Palaeozoic Era, reptiles were probing lands that the amphibians found lethal.

Several early reptile groups had evolved by then. First came small, low-slung creatures such as *Hylonomus* – reptiles collectively named cotylosaurs from a Latin term describing their cup-shaped vertebrae. Cotylosaurs called captorhinomorphs had sharp teeth and hunted insects and amphibians in the coalforest swamps. The much larger, man-length, diadectomorphs, or 'broad-toothed forms', had blunter teeth, perhaps designed to grind up plants. By Permian times, then, there were herbivores (plant-eaters) as well as carnivores (meat-eaters) among the vertebrates.

From the primitive cotylosaur reptiles other kinds branched off, some of which gave rise to mammals. One reptile offshoot was a group called the pelycosaurs. As long as a rhinoceros, they roamed what is now the south-western USA. A skin web, or 'sail', rigged between spiny outgrowths sprouting from the backbones of these long-tailed reptiles, served as a radiator. By altering its angle to the sun, a pelycosaur could speed up the rate at which its body heated up or cooled down – an early instance of cold-blooded animals controlling body temperature, as crocodiles do today.

As Permian time wore on, mammal-like reptiles evolved from the pelycosaurs. Among these were unaggressive plant-eaters like the bulky ('dog-toothed') dicynodonts, which fell prey to rapacious carnivores like *Lycaenops*. Some of the mammal-like reptiles had skulls, teeth, skeletons, stance, and maybe a temperature control system akin to those of their later offshoot the mammals.

By the end of Palaeozoic times, mammal-like reptiles had colonized dry land. But now another group of reptiles was about to give rise to the dinosaurs – beasts destined to make a savage impact on all large, land-based animals.

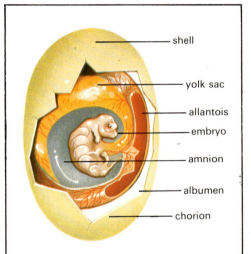

shell
yolk sac
allantois
embryo
amnion
albumen
chorion

A REPTILE'S EGG

Relatively big, well nourished, and protected from drying out, the reptile egg can hatch on land. The tough or hard shell supports the embryo developing inside. Beneath the shell, a membrane called the chorion lets in oxygen and expels carbon dioxide waste. The amnion, another membrane, contains a liquid which cushions the developing embryo and keeps it from drying out. The membrane enclosing the yolk feeds yolk nourishment to the embryo by way of blood vessels. Wastes from the embryo fill a refuse chamber walled by yet another membrane, the allantois.

The First Dinosaurs

More than 200 million years ago,
Ornithosuchus hunted reptiles in
what is now Scotland. The length
of a car, but lighter than a man, it
ran on hind legs, balanced by its
tail. Many experts think it was a
thecodont reptile. Others say it was
an early dinosaur, a small prototype for the largest predators ever
to terrorize wildlife on land.

Early in Mesozoic time, the crocodiles' kin included small, land-based beasts with long hind legs. From them the dinosaurs evolved.

Dinosaurs evolved and spread around the world quite early on in Mesozoic times. There were good reasons for this.

In those distant days almost all the land was warm. The warmth-loving reptiles multiplied and gave rise to many novel groups of creatures, of which the dinosaurs were only one. Then, too, for much of Mesozoic times, the continents as we now know them were gathered together into one great land mass. Dinosaurs evolving in one place were able to spread throughout this vast supercontinent.

The Age of Dinosaurs (or of Reptiles) passed through three phases: the Triassic, Jurassic and Cretaceous periods.

The Triassic Supercontinent

The huge single continent of Triassic times, some 225 million years ago, is referred to by pre-historians as Pangaea. At Pangaea's eastern ends the prehistoric Tethys Ocean separated much of the north (Laurasia) from the southern landmass called Gondwanaland. Meanwhile, the ice sheets that had covered much of Gondwanaland back in late Palaeozoic times had melted. Almost everywhere, the climate was subtropical or tropical. Many lands were desert.

Plants that reproduce by spreading spores need wet soil in which to multiply. Most of the old coal-forest plants were of this type. Those that survived the dry conditions of Triassic times were small and rather scarce. Seed-bearing plants proved better able to survive the dry conditions. Among those that now flourished were conifers, monkey-puzzle trees and palm-like cycads.

Triassic deserts and mountains proved no barriers to land animals. At last these were invading every corner of the continents. Meanwhile new kinds appeared. Hairy, mammal-like reptiles hunted small game. Later, small, shrewlike mammals competed for insect foods with lizards. Then there were early turtles, and rhynchosaurs related to that slow-moving living fossil the tuatara, a creature found only in

In Triassic times the earth's land areas formed one supercontinent (inset map below). Seed-bearing trees like the monkey puzzle (above) grew on dryish soil. Reptiles diversified (below). Mammal-like Lystrosaurus and Thrinaxodon gave way to dinosaurs, including Coelophysis and Plateosaurus. Morganucodon was a true early mammal.

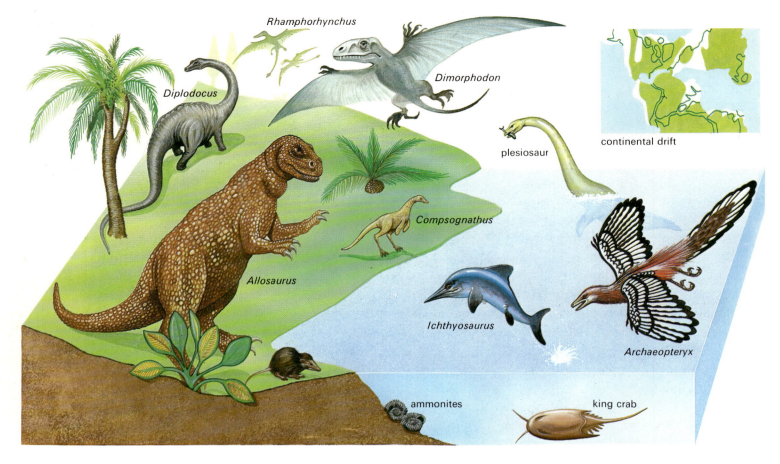

Rhamphorhynchus

Diplodocus

Dimorphodon

plesiosaur

continental drift

Compsognathus

Allosaurus

Ichthyosaurus

Archaeopteryx

ammonites

king crab

Above: The largest animals ever – the great sauropods – appeared during the Jurassic Period. Huge, gentle herbivores like Diplodocus were preyed upon by the flesh-eating Allosaurus. The first known bird, Archaeopteryx, appeared, possibly descended from the small ground-dweller Compsognathus. In the sea swam plesiosaurs and the dolphin-like reptile Ichthyosaurus.

Below: Part of a living cycad, a close relative of land plants that flourished in warm, wet Jurassic landscapes. Living cycads are palm-like, with large leafy crowns from which sprout pine-like cones. They closely resemble the stumpy, unbranched cycadeoids, or bennettitaleans, of Jurassic forests. True cycads were less common than the cycadeoids.

some small islands off the coast of New Zealand. Pre-crocodiles and fierce crocodile-like phytosaurs shared rivers with *Lystrosaurus*, a hippopotamus-like reptile.

Meanwhile other reptiles followed many bony fishes from fresh water to the sea. Reptiles even took to the air. *Kuehneosaurus*, a lizard, had skin flaps which allowed it to glide for short distances.

Then the dinosaurs themselves appeared.

Jurassic Life

The largest and smallest of all dinosaurs lived in the Jurassic Period (200–135 million years ago). Lands, plants, and animals were generally very different from those of the Triassic Period.

Big, if invisibly slow, changes to Pangaea were under way. The northern part of the great land mass began to break away from the southern half. A warm, wet climate produced thick forests of ferns and horsetails beside the rivers, while ginkgoes, conifers and cycads multiplied on drier soils.

Many creatures of Triassic times had died out and been replaced by others. Dinosaurs had almost certainly wiped out the mammal-like reptiles. Mammals themselves remained small and furtive, but modern reptiles were becoming well established. Ichthyosaurs and plesiosaurs – big, aquatic reptiles – hunted fishes in the seas. By the close of the

Jurassic Period, birds and other flying animals derived from reptiles were winging through the skies.

The Cretaceous Scene

Dinosaurs became most plentiful and diverse in Cretaceous times (135–65 million years ago). It was during this period that the world took on a modern look.

During the Cretaceous Period the two great land masses began to break up into the continents we know today. Bit by bit they drifted toward their modern positions. Shallow seas spread across part of the continents, dividing up the land surfaces even more. Here and there the great moving plates in the earth's crust clashed and flung up mountain chains, which brought climatic changes to the lands on either side of them. On the whole, world climates cooled.

A cooling climate favoured the spread of flowering plants – plants whose seeds usually grow inside a protective casing called a fruit. Magnolias, oaks and aspens were among the trees of modern type that now appeared.

Cut adrift on separate continents in a variety of climates, the land animals underwent considerable changes. In the northern continents a wealth of two-legged and four-legged dinosaurs evolved. Many were designed to browse upon

Above: Magnolia blossoms have cone-like centres suggesting that these plants came from some cone-bearing ancestors. Magnolias were among the first flowering plants to bloom, late in the Mesozoic Era. Seeds protected by an outer casing gave flowering plants a better chance than cycads of thriving in the cool climates of late Cretaceous northern lands.

Below: Dinosaurs still dominated the land in late Cretaceous times, when the continents were moving towards their modern positions. Triceratops, Tyrannosaurus and Parasaurolophus were all new. Huge aquatic reptiles still swam in shallow seas. Mammals stayed small and timid. But birds now shared the sky with the skin-winged pterosaurs.

the leaves of conifers or flowering plants. Others preyed upon the browsers. Mammals stayed small and insignificant. The seas still held numbers of great reptiles that preyed on fishes or on one another. A broadening variety of birds not very different from some alive today shared the air with giant skin-winged gliding animals, the biggest airborne creatures ever.

But with the ending of Cretaceous times, the dinosaurs and many other ancient forms of life disappeared. (See page 78.)

How Dinosaurs Began

The reptile line that led to dinosaurs was well established by Triassic times. From small, lizard-like beasts, two reptile branches had diverged. From one would come modern lizards and snakes. From the other – the thecodont ('socket-toothed') branch – would arise the archosaurs ('ruling reptiles'). These were the crocodiles, dinosaurs and flying reptiles.

One beast foreshadowing the crocodiles was *Proterosuchus*, which lived in lakes and rivers preying upon fish, amphibians and reptiles. *Proterosuchus* had a sprawling walk, rather like an early amphibian; but its descendants' bodies altered as they adapted to their lives in water. They gained a powerful, flattened tail with which they swam. Then, too, their hind legs lengthened and were realigned to thrust straight down and backward.

One line of such water-living animals gave rise to modern crocodilians. From another reptile line, about 225 million years ago, came *Euparkeria*. *Euparkeria* resembled a small, lightweight, long-limbed crocodile, under a metre (three feet) in length, but it lived on land. It walked on all fours but ran on its hind legs only, its long, strong tail balancing the front part of the body.

By 200 million years ago, such small, speedy, insect-eating reptiles had fathered beasts like *Ornithosuchus* pictured on page 24. *Ornitho-*

Top: Proterosuchus lived in Triassic swamps, preying on other reptiles, amphibians and fish. Like its amphibian ancestors, it had limbs that stuck out sideways so that it sprawled. Such early archosaurs gave rise to the crocodilians and dinosaurs.

Above: Modern crocodilians, unlike their reptile ancestor Proterosuchus, can raise their bodies well off the ground to run on land. When the dinosaurs evolved, they too were better designed to move easily and quickly on land than their sprawling ancestors.

Right: Euparkeria was an archosaur up to one metre (three feet) long. It walked on all fours but could run fast on its hind legs. The formidable flesh-eating dinosaurs probably evolved from Euparkeria. Coelophysis (below right) may have evolved from a near relative of Euparkeria. From lightweight Coelophysis sprang the coelurosaurs, nimble hunters of small prey.

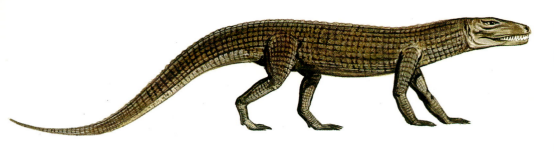

Left: The long, low reptile Ticinosuchus, reconstructed from fossils found in the Swiss Alps. This relative of Euparkeria was an archosaur that walked on all fours. Ticinosuchus was only three metres (nine feet) long and had a carnivore's sharp teeth. But it probably gave rise to the largest of all dinosaurs, the plant-eating sauropods.

suchus resembled big, two-legged, meat-eating dinosaurs called carnosaurs that also appeared.

Meanwhile a more graceful, agile group of predatory two-legged creatures was in the making. *Coelophysis*, a true dinosaur which lived in North America, was the first of these coelurosaurs, as they were called.

Speedy or well armed carnivorous dinosaurs and other archosaurs largely changed the shape of life on land. When Triassic times began, mammal-like flesh-eating reptiles had been all-powerful. By the time this period was over, the archosaurs had almost wiped them out. With the flesh-eating mammal-like reptiles, too, went most of the plant-eating mammal-like reptiles they had preyed upon.

But these herbivores may have been at least partly shouldered out by peaceful competition for their food supply – competition provided by the first plant-eating dinosaurs. Fortunately for the flesh-eaters, their plant-eating cousins came along in time to fill the food gap left by the disappearing mammal-like reptiles.

Ancestors of Giants

From one group of plant-eating dinosaurs sprang the sauropods – the largest-ever animals to walk on land. Just how these giants evolved remains uncertain. But, like the coelurosaurs and carnosaurs, they too very likely came from a small beast resembling *Euparkeria*.

Many scientists believe that the sauropods' likeliest ancestor was *Ticinosuchus*. This long, low, carnivorous reptile of Triassic times

One of the first big plant-eating dinosaurs was Plateosaurus, a bulky herbivore about 6 metres (20 feet) long. Plateosaur herds roamed Triassic lands in search of vegetation. The beasts may have walked as quadrupeds but reared up to feed.

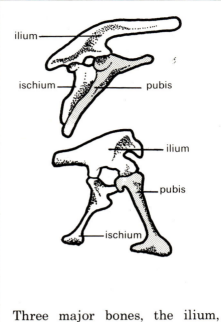

Three major bones, the ilium, ischium and pubis, make up the hip girdle of a dinosaur. In saurischian dinosaurs the ischium was angled backwards, the pubis forwards. In ornithischian dinosaurs, the pubis lay parallel to the ischium.

One of the first ornithischian dinosaurs was little Fabrosaurus from southern Africa. No longer than a large lizard, this slightly built dinosaur with long hind legs at first glance resembled the carnivorous coelurosaurs. But it plainly cropped leaves with its horny beak and mashed them with teeth designed as grinders. Scientists differ about how such small dinosaurs kept their bodies warm and still had enough energy to run around.

held its body well off the ground. But unlike *Euparkeria*, it walked and ran around on all four legs. *Ticinosuchus* evidently fathered a group of dinosaurs with long necks and small teeth, ill-suited to tackling large prey. These beasts included *Thecodontosaurus*, arguably the first dinosaur to eat plants as well as animals.

By late Triassic times such small plant-eating dinosaurs had given rise to much larger ones. Best known of these was *Plateosaurus*, which lived in Europe about 200 million years ago. *Plateosaurus* differed from flesh-eating dinosaurs in several ways. Six metres (20 feet) in length, it was considerably bigger and bulkier. Probably it usually bore its weight on all four limbs. But its hind legs were longer and stronger than its front legs, and *Plateosaurus* doubtless reared up to bite off leaves growing high off the ground.

Lizard- or Bird-hipped?

The flesh-eating and plant-eating dinosaurs so far described were built for leading very different lives.

But they shared one distinctive feature: a similar type of hip girdle. This earns the general name saurischians ('lizard-hipped') for both the plant-eating sauropods and their flesh-eating cousins – the theropods, as the carnosaurs and coelurosaurs are called collectively.

Triassic times saw, too, the rise of a second major group of dinosaurs. These ornithischian ('bird-hipped') beasts had a hip girdle design clearly different from that of all saurischians. Ornithischians also had distinctive beak-like jaws. At the same time their ankle bones were built so like those of the saurischians that many scientists feel sure both of the major groups of dinosaur sprang from one ancestor.

The first known ornithischian was *Fabrosaurus*, a metre-long (three-foot) dinosaur with long back legs and short front ones. *Fabrosaurus* may have run on its hind legs but walked on all fours, like *Euparkeria*. In time, there were both four-legged and predominantly two-legged ornithischians. But unlike some saurischians, all of them were vegetarians.

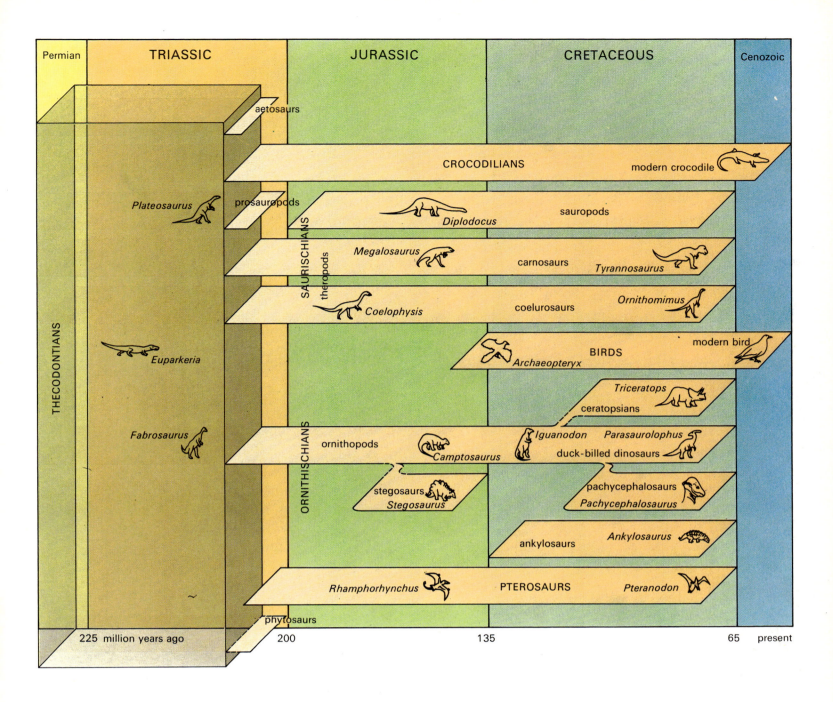

The main branches of the archosaur 'family tree', showing when each group of animals evolved and became extinct. Birds and crocodilians are the only groups stemming from the archosaurs that have survived.

WARM-BLOODED DINOSAURS?

Some scientists believe that dinosaurs, unlike modern reptiles, were warm blooded and much faster-moving than previously thought. They think it is possible that plant-eating *Plateosaurus* was the first warm-blooded dinosaur.

Birds and mammals of today keep a constant body temperature by producing heat within their muscles. Modern reptiles, however, rely on the sun's heat to warm themselves – they are cold blooded.

Dinosaurs had relatively long legs and an erect limb posture. All living long-legged creatures travel quickly; therefore, it is argued, the dinosaurs must have been capable of quite a high maximum speed. Only a warm-blooded animal is capable of high speeds for more than a few seconds. And, unlike reptiles but like modern mammals (including Man), the dinosaurs had a secondary palate which allowed them to breathe while eating. A warm-blooded animal has to breathe continuously, so this adaptation would seem unnecessary in a cold-blooded creature.

Dinosaur bones are found to contain many blood vessels, rather like those of a modern mammal. Modern reptiles' bones are not like this. The mammalian type of bone is thought to be necessary for a high metabolic rate – for a quick-moving, warm-blooded animal.

Gentle Giants

Melanorosaurus
12 metres (40 feet)

Apatosaurus
25 metres (80 feet)

Cetiosaurus
18 metres (60 feet)

Brachiosaurus
26 metres (85 feet)

Man

Man contrasted with four giant dinosaurs. The Triassic forerunner of the sauropods, Melanorosaurus, was as long as seven men lying end to end. The Jurassic sauropod Cetiosaurus measured half as long again. Apatosaurus grew even larger; but Brachiosaurus was the most massive dinosaur of all.

New discoveries about the biggest-ever dinosaurs have changed our notions of how they lived.

Lush forests sprouted in many places in the warm, wet climates of Jurassic times. This wealth of plant food helped the large plant-eating dinosaurs to multiply and branch out in new, colossal forms. Some weighed 50 tonnes or more, and measured several bus-lengths. For size and weight, these mighty sauropods outstripped any land animal that came before or after them. Giants among the dinosaurs, their kind persisted right through the Mesozoic Era. But they were never more abundant than in Jurassic times, and nowhere more plentiful than in North America.

One of the largest land animals ever, Cetiosaurus was nearly as long as two touring coaches and as heavy as three elephants. Lengthy, pillar-like front legs and a giraffe-like neck bore the giant's head roof high.

Most got their scientific, Latin, names from real or supposed resemblances to familiar living animals, or from some special feature of their body, or imagined way of life. 'Sauropod', the very name of this whole group of dinosaurs, means 'lizard-footed' (or 'reptile-footed') – a reference to the five-toed feet that many sauropods had in common with today's lizards.

The 'Whale Lizard'

The first fossil finds of sauropods came in England. Whale-sized fossil ribs dug up near Oxford in the 1830s led scientists to name their prehistoric owner *Cetiosaurus*: 'whale lizard'. *Cetiosaurus* was as heavy as three elephants combined and measured 18 metres (60 feet) from head to tail. People wrongly guessed that this lengthy sauropod had swum around in the sea.

Another prehistoric titan was *Camarasaurus*, or 'chambered lizard', so-called from the hollow chambers in its backbone. *Camarasaurus* grew almost as large as *Cetiosaurus*. Both lived in what are now Europe and North America. Overshadowing both these giants was *Brachiosaurus*, or 'arm lizard', so named from its relatively long front legs. Some individuals may have weighed an unbelievable 100 tonnes, equal to 20 large elephants. *Brachiosaurus* was the heaviest dinosaur of them all.

Diplodocus' skull, with its peg-like teeth, was tiny. This huge sauropod had a brain the size of a kitten's.

ELEPHANT OR ALLIGATOR?

Most *Diplodocus* models show this monster standing upright like an elephant. In 1910, however, America's Oliver P. Hay argued that it must have sprawled as a resting alligator does.

But W. J. Holland, creator of the best-known 'upright' model, showed that the deep ribcage of a creeping *Diplodocus* would have gouged a great rut in the ground. Finds of fossil footprints later proved that Holland had been right. Today it is thought that *Diplodocus* not only stood upright to graze on foliage high off the ground, but that this 27-metre (88-foot) giant could balance on its hind legs to reach even higher into the trees.

Right: Diplodocus' leg and thigh bones were large and heavy to support its great weight. But its backbone was surprisingly light, for each bone was hollowed out.

One giant, *Apatosaurus*, was once known as *Brontosaurus* ('thunder lizard') because the man who named it thought its feet must have thumped thunderously on the ground as this colossus strode along. *Apatosaurus* was in fact less than one-third as heavy as the biggest of the brachiosaurs.

Much lighter than *Brachiosaurus* yet even longer was *Diplodocus* ('double beam'). At up to 27 metres (88 feet) *Diplodocus* was the longest-ever land animal. Its name comes from its tail bones, each featuring two bars and seemingly designed with skids to safeguard blood vessels housed inside the tail while it was dragging on the ground. *Barosaurus* ('heavy lizard'), another giant, was among *Diplodocus'* huge closer relatives.

Most sauropods lived in Jurassic times. But some flourished in the next, Cretaceous, period. These dinosaurs looked rather like smaller versions of *Diplodocus*. They penetrated almost all parts of the world.

Giant Proportions
Sauropod species varied in their weights, lengths and proportions. But all were massive, and all shared the same basic plan. Four legs as thick as tree trunks propped up a mighty torso from which a long neck at the front and a long tail at the rear projected like booms cantilevered from a crane.

Bone 'girders' provided bodily support. Leg bones were massive, solid objects. The hind-leg bones linked up with a colossal hip girdle anchoring the muscles powering these limbs, which supported most of their owner's weight. Long, flat shoulder blades and other bones formed a forward-end assembly, helping to bear muscles powering the relatively short front limbs.

Strong yet lightweight, the backbone worked like the steel span of a cantilever bridge. In contrast with the solid, heavy leg bones, the backbone contained hollow, air-filled spaces, similar to the hollow bones of birds. These simply helped to cut down weight. Vertebrae interlocking on a ball and socket principle gave the backbone flexibility. Long spines jutting upward from the vertebrae afforded muscle-holds, and a cable-like ligament cradled in the V-shaped dip of each spiny outcrop helped the beast to lift and drop its neck much as a crane-operator lifts and drops his boom.

The boom's 'business end' was a head larger than a horse's, yet tiny for so huge a beast. Skull finds suggest that, bulk for bulk, sauropods had the smallest brains of any backboned creature. Some, at least, had a brain no larger than a kitten's. They had big eyes, but relatively weak jaws and few teeth. Another curious feature of sauropods was the position of their nostrils high up on their heads.

From fossil sauropod skeletons, then, we can build up a rough picture of the size and shape of their bodies. But experts still argue about just how some of the pieces fitted together or how they worked. It is worth looking more closely at these problems in order to understand how the giant dinosaurs moved, ate, and multiplied themselves – in other words how they actually lived.

Land or Water Dwellers?
From the first finds of the 1830s, most scientists concluded that the giant sauropods had been more at home in water than on land. Many details of their structure seemed to point that way.

First, it seemed far-fetched to think that a creature weighing so

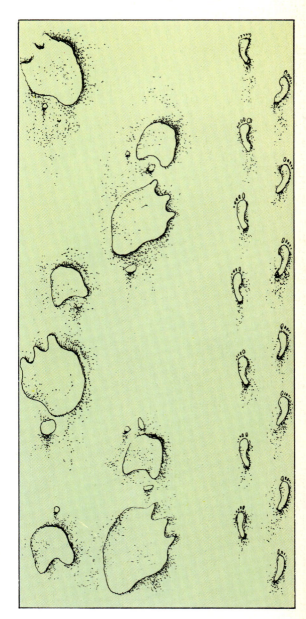

Above: The footprints of a striding man compared with sauropod tracks made over 150 million years ago in Texan mud. The mud later turned to rock in which the fossil prints have been preserved. Front feet made the smaller prints, while the hind feet punched holes as wide and deep as washtubs.

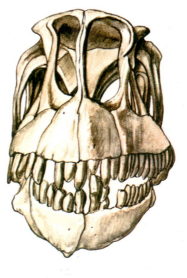

Two views of a Camarasaurus skull show a surprisingly delicate structure for so huge a beast. This nerve centre of a mighty sauropod was hardly longer than a man's foot. The upper part was roofed with bone but the sides were pierced by windows framed with bony struts. Bony sockets show that the beast had large eyes and nostrils. Most of the skull's weight was concentrated in the jaws. In relation to their body size, the sauropods had smaller brains than those of any other backboned animal.

many tonnes could stand and walk around on land without its great weight crushing its own leg bones.

Water, though, would have buoyed up a sauropod's vast bulk. The hollow, lightweight bones of its back and neck would have helped the upper part of its body to float. The solid, heavy leg bones would have served as ballast, like the lead soles on divers' boots, to keep the creature upright. And nostrils high up on the head offered another hint that sauropods lived in water.

Proof that sauropods actually swam came from fossil footprints found in prehistoric mud in Texas. The prints showed front feet only. These had pressed lightly on the bed of an ancient lake or river as a brontosaur used its forelimbs to pole itself along. Meanwhile its hollow backbone and gas in the intestines buoyed up the long hind limbs. The impression of a single hind foot showed where the beast had kicked off to change direction.

Scientists thus built up a picture of the sauropods as wading and swimming in warm Jurassic swamps, lakes and rivers. Only there, it seemed, would these placid herbivores find the kinds of food they needed. What these foods had been seemed plain from studies of the sauropods' fossil teeth, shaped like pegs, spoons or pencils. Many experts considered these too weak to have ground up tough land plants, but suitable for snatching mouthfuls of soft, lush water vegetation.

They thus came to imagine sauropods living a watery life out of reach of the fierce carnosaurs that tried to prey upon them. Sometimes, of course, the giants had to come ashore, to lay eggs or because their pool dried up; but the great defenceless brutes would have soon sought safety in water once again.

Now, though, all these notions have been seriously questioned. Palaeontologists increasingly believe that sauropods lived not in swamps or lakes but with their washtub-sized feet planted on land.

Many arguments support this new idea. For instance, sauropods

Below: A herd of Barosaurus, their young protected in the middle, plod heavily through the Jurassic landscape. Goose-sized Compsognathus dart out of the way of their elephant-like feet. African elephants (above) hold clues to the way the sauropods once lived. The massive bodies, pillar-like legs, and herding habits of these largest living land animals remind us of those giants of the past.

were built more like that huge land animal the elephant, than like the bulky but water-dwelling hippopotamus. The elephant's legs bear its weight on land, provided that it stands and moves stiff legged, instead of bending freely at the knees and elbows like a hippopotamus. Similarly, fresh calculations now show that a single sauropod limb could have borne a load of several tonnes. A hippopotamus can walk on land, but its short legs and shallow ribs are better suited to a life spent in the water. Then, too, its splayed toes help it stand on soft, wet mud better than the short, stumpy toes possessed by both elephants and sauropods.

Many scientists now think that the sauropods' light, hollow backbones may not have been for buoyancy, but just to help to cut down body weight on land. Lying down and standing up again would have been laborious tasks for sauropods. But they may have slept standing, like elephants and horses.

The Sauropod Diet

How, though, did they feed? A once-widespread notion held that sauropods walked on lake beds, only their eyes and nostrils breaking the surface as they browsed on soft, aquatic

A female Camarasaurus stands guard as her baby hatches from its egg. We can only guess that such events occurred. The mother may have simply left her egg to hatch untended, warmed by the sun. We do know, however, what the hatchling would have looked like. A rare fossil find reveals that a baby Camarasaurus had a relatively larger head and shorter neck than an adult.

plants. Studies now show that the water pressure on a *Brachiosaurus* standing 12 metres (40 feet) deep would have crushed its lungs, and either swamped the lungs with escaping blood or prevented blood from getting to the brain. In any case it seems unlikely that there were enough plants for them to eat in deep waters. On land, though, there were plants in plenty. Put the sauropods on land, and we can see that their long necks could have served a simpler and more likely purpose than as parts of living periscopes and snorkels. Like a giraffe, a long-necked dinosaur could have browsed on tree-top leaves and shoots too high for other beasts to reach.

Sauropods' teeth may have been weak compared with those of cows and sheep, but some fossil teeth that have been found were plainly worn down by gnawing something hard – perhaps the starchy substances in cycad tree trunks. And though sauropods lacked the grinding cheek teeth of a horse, they may have had 'millstones' in their stomachs. Like crocodiles and birds, sauropods may have swallowed

rough-edged stones especially to aid digestion. When these stones wore smooth inside them, they would have spat them out and swallowed more. (Smooth stones have been found near fossil sauropods.)

Calculating how much food sauropods got through daily is guesswork. A big one would have needed a tonne of leaves a day to power its body – if its body worked like an elephant's. But sauropods were not mammals, and they probably needed much less food because their bodies used up energy at a slower rate. Otherwise it is hard to see how they could have crammed leaves down their narrow throats fast enough to stay alive.

Herds of Giants

Even so, a hungry sauropod would have quickly stripped the tender leaves and shoots from many trees. Imagine then, the ravages of a whole herd of these giant dinosaurs. For there is good evidence that the sauropods did not live solitary lives, but moved about in groups. Careful study of fossil tracks discovered in a Texan quarry revealed that one day, many millions of years ago, 23 brontosaurs had passed that way

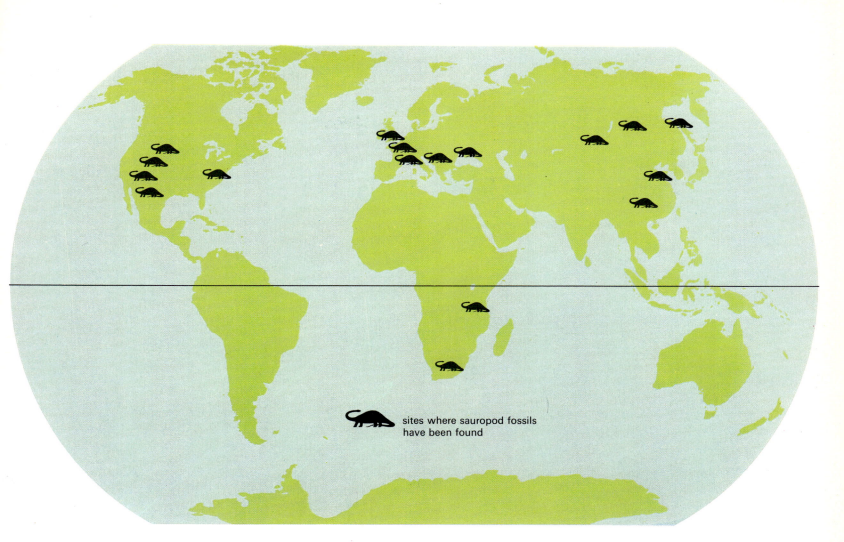

sites where sauropod fossils
have been found

together. Another group of fossil tracks revealed 15 brontosaurs following a slowly plodding leader. Curiously, the beasts left no traces of their huge tails dragging behind them. Some scientists suggest that they may have held their tails stiffly off the ground.

These collective movements in the same direction suggest a common purpose. The likely explanation must surely be that the dinosaurs had eaten all the food that they could find in one locality, and now were on the march to find new browsing grounds.

To help them in this search they may have had a keen sense of smell. Many scientists now think that the large size of sauropod nostrils may indicate a highly developed sense of smell.

A keen sense of smell may also have helped to warn the herd of danger from lurking carnosaurs. Lacking any obvious defensive weapons, threatened sauropods may have tried to flee. But the idea that they found safety in deep water is suspect. For the carnosaurs could well have chased them, swimming with powerful backward thrusts of their great hind legs.

Instead of fleeing, the members of the herd most probably drew close together, perhaps with big,

old, tough-skinned bulls to guard the flanks. The relatively thin-skinned and very vulnerable young sauropods may have huddled within this living wall. If a carnosaur attacked the herd, big bulls may have reared up and delivered crushing blows with their forelimbs.

Sauropods found safety in the herd. But how they fought we can only guess at. In the same way we can only guess that they guarded their young. This theory may appear far-fetched. Most sauropods seem to have laid eggs instead of giving birth to young in the manner of the elephant. The mothers may have simply deposited the eggs in sand and left them for the sun to hatch. Most living reptiles act this way. But some snakes and crocodilians guard their eggs until they hatch. Maybe sauropods did too. It would certainly have greatly helped the babies' chances of survival.

Sauropod family life remains a puzzle, but we can at least now picture how and where these dinosaurs ate and travelled. We see them blazing trails through forests, and browsing on leaves high in the trees. Sometimes, they may have swum and wallowed to drown parasites or stop their dry hides cracking, but we are now almost certain that their home was on dry land.

Above: Sauropod fossils have been found at numerous sites in Asia, Africa, Europe and North America. Brachiosaurus, the heaviest dinosaur of them all, roamed all these continents. Diplodocus, the longest animal ever, was confined to North America.

Fearful Fangs

Terrifying carnosaurs and bird-like coelurosaurs were the lions and jackals of the Age of Dinosaurs.

The word 'dinosaur' may conjure up an image of a huge, slow sauropod. But perhaps more often, fed by cinema and TV re-creations, we imagine the terrible teeth of *Tyrannosaurus*, revealed in a mighty roar as this fierce monster towers over a helpless victim.

Tyrannosaurus did not, in fact, appear until the Cretaceous Period – late in the dinosaur story. But a complete line of flesh-eating dinosaurs, or carnosaurs, flourished throughout the Age of Dinosaurs. Some weighed no more than a saddle horse. Others were at least as heavy as an elephant and longer than a touring coach. All were built on the same broad plan. Two huge, muscular hind legs bore the whole weight of the body. The front limbs were small. The tail was long and strong. A short, thick neck supported a massive head. The jaws held huge, sharp teeth, and from the toes grew claws like sickles. Smaller claws projected from the 'fingers'.

Carnosaurs included the biggest land predators that ever hunted. They seem to have evolved to fight and kill far bigger prey than any animals now found on land. Their victims were the huge plant-eating dinosaurs.

Families of Flesh-eaters

The two main carnosaur families were megalosaurs and tyrannosaurs. Megalosaurs were medium to large carnosaurs; tyrannosaurs were all large. Megalosaurs came first, appearing early in the Jurassic Period.

By a curious coincidence, one of the earliest megalosaurs was also the first fossil dinosaur to be re-corded. The Reverend Dr Robert Plot pictured a *Megalosaurus* thigh bone in a book 300 years ago. But its true identity remained unknown until the 19th century. *Megalosaurus* ('large reptile') grew up to 9 metres (30 feet) long. It had powerful weapons in the form of pointed, curved and saw-edged teeth like penknife blades with strong, thick bases. Powerful muscles worked the jaws.

Megalosaurus balanced its long bulky body on powerful three-toed hind limbs whose thick, solid bones helped to bear the body's weight. The front limbs were too small for use in walking, and only three of the five fingers were well developed.

Remains of dozens of *Megalosaurus* species have been found. Their fossil bones or footprints crop up as far apart as Portugal and Greenland.

Some of the fossils show trends toward new forms. For instance, one species found in Dorset had spines 25 cm (10 inches) long growing upward from its backbone. From such beasts may have come *Spinosaurus*, a 12-metre-long (39-foot) carnosaur that lived in late Cretaceous Egypt. *Spinosaurus* had spines longer than a man's body. A web of skin was probably stretched between them as in that ancient reptile carnivore *Dimetrodon*. By turning its side into the early morning sun, *Spinosaurus* might have warmed up fast enough to hunt other cold-blooded animals before they were warm enough to be alert. At noon, *Spinosaurus* would have stood with tail or head facing the sun, keeping cool by losing heat from its built-in radiator. This ex-

Above: A carnosaur's tooth, shown actual size, from late Jurassic rocks in Tanzania. A curved blade with saw-tooth edges, this was an ideal tool for slicing huge chunks of flesh from the carcasses of prey.

Left: Fossil megalosaur footprints show up as damp dips in the dry, cracked floor of a quarry. Well preserved tracks show that megalosaurs probably walked with their toes turned in.

Opposite page: Megalosaurus, a carnosaur, browses on the massive body of a sauropod, Cetiosaurus. Carnosaurs had claws and fangs enabling them to kill unarmoured dinosaurs much larger than themselves.

planation holds good only if *Spinosaurus*, too, were not warm blooded as birds and mammals are.

The 'Leaping Reptile'

But the most formidable megalosaur was *Allosaurus* ('leaping reptile'), also known as *Antrodemus*. *Allosaurus* shared late Jurassic North America with the vast, peaceful sauropods that it preyed upon. Its whole body was up to three metres (nine feet) longer than *Megalosaurus*'s.

Allosaurus's great jaws bore an arsenal of blade-like fangs, and the jaws' huge gape helped *Allosaurus* to bolt great chunks of flesh. Only 'windows' in the skull made this massive structure light enough to be supported by the creature's short, thick neck. Each forelimb bore three big 'fingers' armed with long claws. Jaws and claws simultaneously savaged *Allosaurus*'s victims.

King of the Carnivores

The biggest carnosaurs of all were the tyrannosaurs of late Cretaceous times. Best known among these monsters was North America's *Tyrannosaurus rex* ('king of the tyrant reptiles'). The name seems apt enough. From tail tip to snout, *Tyrannosaurus* spanned up to 14 metres (47 feet). The creature would have dwarfed even *Allosaurus*, if that carnosaur had been still living. If *Tyrannosaurus* stood upright, it would have been tall enough to peer into the upstairs windows of a house. Like the other carnosaurs, *Tyrannosaurus* usually walked with head held low and thrust forward. *Tyrannosaurus* held its heavy tail up off the ground, like a balancing rod.

This carnosaur weighed more than most African bull elephants. Each of its immensely powerful hind legs bore perhaps a four-tonne load – more than the entire weight of a white rhinoceros. The three big forward-pointing toes bore claws as long as carving knives. *Tyrannosaurus* had a head in keeping with its terrifying size. The long, narrow skull measured just over a metre (four feet) and each eye socket was big enough to hold a human head. Avenues of sabre-like teeth – some nearly the length of a man's hand – lined the jaws.

Two tyrannosaurids challenge each other for the half-eaten remains of a hadrosaur. No flesh-eating beasts that ever lived on land were larger or more menacing than these monsters of late Cretaceous North America. Among plant-eating dinosaurs, only the most fleet-footed, heavily armoured or formidably horned species survived encounters with them.

A struggle to the death between the agile predator Velociraptor and the herbivore Protoceratops. Their fossil skeletons were found 'frozen' in the midst of the struggle, when some untimely death overtook them. No one knows why both dinosaurs died together.

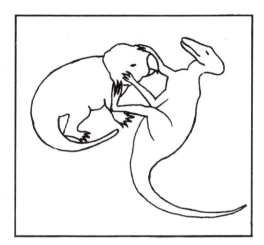

Even more extraordinary than its huge bulk and armoury of fangs and claws were *Tyrannosaurus*'s tiny arms. The monster's forelimbs were probably as long and muscular as human legs. Each arm bore two 'fingers' tipped with big claws. But seen against the great bulk of the creature's body, the arms appeared absurdly puny. They were too small to help it kill its prey; too short to shovel food into the mouth. What, then, were they used for?

One ingenious suggestion would have it that *Tyrannosaurus* rested in a doglike pose, with hind legs underneath its body, and head stretched out along the ground. To stand up it pressed down with its long hind legs. But this would have tended to make its head slide forward. So, it is suggested, *Tyrannosaurus* may have dug its front claws into the ground to stop this happening, and thus to help it rise.

Even when it walked, *Tyrannosaurus* may have seemed ungainly. Studies of its fossil skeleton suggest that the tyrant waddled somewhat like a giant duck. Each time it raised a foot to take a step the tail swung to one side to help it balance.

Predators or Scavengers?

Some scientists believe that the giant was a cold-blooded, sluggish reptile, never capable of more than a slow, plodding walk. They believe, too, that *Tyrannosaurus* lacked the energy to wage a long, ferocious battle with the duck-billed or horned dinosaurs that it very likely fed upon.

Supposed proofs of this lethargy include the unworn teeth of a fossil *Gorgosaurus* – a similar tyrannosaur from North America. One expert has suggested that such carnosaurs were really scavengers, living off the soft flesh of dinosaurs they found already dead.

Yet the carnosaurs' great arsenal of weapons makes this seem unlikely. Other fossil clues back up a belief in carnosaurs as active hunters. Fossil footprints found in Texas show an *Allosaurus* hot on the trail of its victim – a huge brontosaur.

Then, too, finds of fossil carnosaurs are far scarcer than those of the plant-eating dinosaurs they fed upon. This implies that it took many herbivores to feed one carnosaur. Some scientists think that such a large appetite might suggest that carnosaurs were warm-blooded and their bodies always 'energized' – more like lions than lizards. However, there may be other explanations for the fact that fossil carnosaurs are rather rare. It may be, for

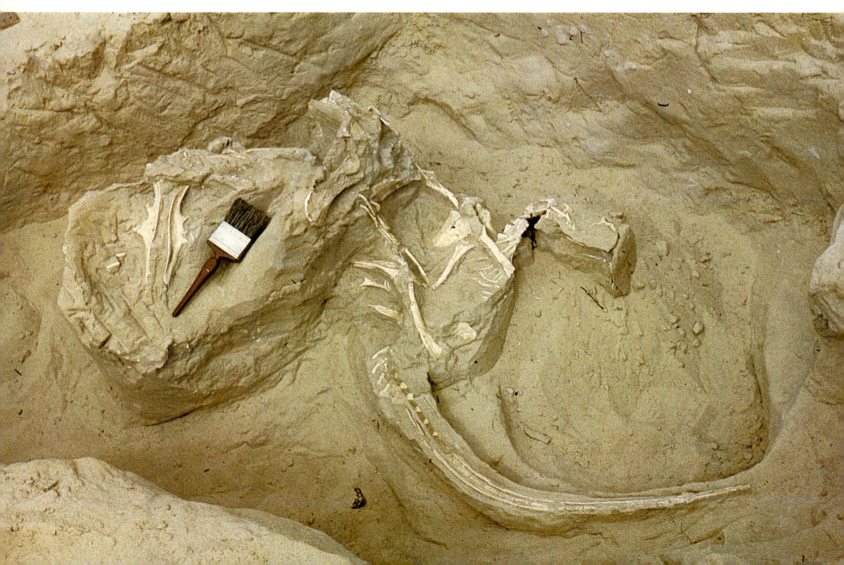

TERRIBLE CLAWS

A whole new group of carnivorous dinosaurs came to light in 1964. In that year, in Montana's early Cretaceous rocks, the American palaeontologist John Ostrom discovered fossil bones of *Deinonychus* ('terrible claw'). *Deinonychus* had been a relatively small and lightweight killer, under three metres (nine feet) long, yet it was possibly more lethal than the largest carnosaurs. *Deinonychus* sprinted after prey on long, muscular hind legs, balanced by a tail incorporating bony rods as stiffeners. The second toe of each hind foot remained off the ground, and bore a huge, curved claw. The arms were long and clawed fingers dangled from them.

Deinonychus evidently raked a victim savagely with one hind leg, its huge claw slashing downward in a semicircle to inflict great gaping gashes in the hide of its prey.

instance, that the carnosaurs lived longer than the herbivores.

There is clearer proof that predatory dinosaurs grappled fiercely with their prey. In 1971 palaeontologists discovered two fossil dinosaurs that evidently died in combat. One was the plant-eating *Protoceratops*. The other was *Velociraptor* ('swift robber'), a long-legged predatory dinosaur with grasping hands.

The Coelurosaurs

Velociraptor belonged not to the huge carnosaurs, but to those much smaller and more agile theropods, the coelurosaurs. While carnosaurs were grappling with big game, the coelurosaurs chased small game in the undergrowth. Carnosaurs were heavyweight predators, with solid, robust bones to bear their weight. But the slim, hollow bones of the coelurosaurs ensured that these dinosaurs remained lightweight and relatively small.

During the Jurassic Period they came in rich variety. Among the largest was *Ornitholestes* or 'bird robber'. The scientist who named it thought that the clawed 'fingers' on its long arms had been used for catching agile prey, perhaps even birds. We should really call this creature *Coelurus* from fossil finds made and named more than 20 years before the *Ornitholestes* fossils were christened. Both sets of fossils turned out to belong to the same kind of dinosaur.

Coelurus (or *Ornitholestes*) was somewhat longer than a man, but weighed much less. It had a small, low skull, and a long neck balanced by an even longer tail. *Coelurus* ran on its long, strong, hind legs, with its neck outstretched. Its arms were longer in relation to its legs than those of carnosaurs, and fingers tipped with strong, curved claws made useful weapons.

Imagine *Coelurus* darting through bushes too thick for carnosaurs to penetrate. There it would have snapped up lizards, and mouse-sized mammals. Maybe it surprised and seized startled birds and pterosaurs. *Coelurus* quite likely also scav-

enged, tearing flesh from the carnosaurs' leftovers, much as jackals profit from a lion's kill today.

Small though they were, such dinosaurs dwarfed the little coelurosaurs called *Compsognathus*. Some kinds were scarcely bigger than a hen. No known dinosaur came tinier than that. *Compsognathus* resembled a slender, agile, wingless bird, but sharp little teeth studded the jaws of its fragile, finger-length skull, and its forelimbs bore three-clawed fingers.

Small, sprinting coelurosaurs like this plainly used up energy at a rapid rate. Like carnosaurs, coelurosaurs very likely had some built-in mechanism to keep their bodies at the high temperature needed for sustained swift movement. This may have made them warm blooded in the way that birds and mammals are.

Coelurosaurs lost heat energy relatively faster than big dinosaurs because their surface area was much larger in relation to their total body size. Possibly some coelurosaurs reduced heat loss by evolving an

Above: This beautifully preserved fossil of Archaeopteryx clearly shows the feathers that clothed its body.

Several coelurosaurs – small, predatory dinosaurs – figure in this late Jurassic scene from Europe. Two kinds of hen-sized Compsognathus (one with flippers) hunt at the water's edge. Nearby, Ornitholestes, a larger coelurosaur, speeds in search of prey. Archaeopteryx, an early, crow-sized bird, may have evolved from a coelurosaur.

outer insulating layer – a layer made of scales that grew abnormally: each scale fraying into dozens of split ends. Thousands of interlocking frayed scales would trap a thin layer of warm air against a creature's body. Such a layer could help to stop heat leaking out, thus conserving energy required for rapid movement. When deformed scales like these grow on birds we call them 'feathers'. From feathered coelurosaurs it may indeed have been but a short evolutionary step to the first birds.

Birds and 'Bird Mimics'

Much of this is guesswork. Feathers are usually too fragile to survive as fossils. But the first known birds certainly fluttered around at the same time and in the same place as *Compsognathus*. What is more, their skeletons were remarkably alike. Birds, then, very likely evolved from dinosaurs. Some scientists even argue that birds *are* dinosaurs – and thus the sole survivors of the dinosaur line.

sites where flesh-eating dinosaur fossils have been found

A world map shows where the flesh-eating dinosaurs lived. Early carnosaurs inhabited South Africa and Europe. Megalosaurs roamed Europe, Asia, Africa and the Americas. East Asia and North America were tyrannosaurid strongholds. The slightly-built coelurosaurs were at home in all these lands, and several species thrived in what is now Australia.

Ornithomimus, the 'bird mimic', was one of several big, bird-like dinosaurs of late Cretaceous North America. The equivalent of a modern ostrich, Ornithomimus could run fast if chased by predators. It may have pecked fruit from bushes with its toothless, bird-like beak, assisted by the three long 'fingers' on each hand. These also could have served to dig out buried dinosaur eggs – a special delicacy.

The first recorded bird was *Archaeopteryx* ('ancient wing'). *Archaeopteryx* was the size of a crow, with a long reptilian tail, a beak with teeth, and clawed fingers projecting forward from its wings. It lacked strong flight muscles, and may have merely clawed its way up trees, then glided down. But before the Mesozoic Era ended, *Archaeopteryx* had given rise to true flying birds, some resembling modern terns and divers.

Imagine that a time machine has turned the clock back to the North America of 70 million years ago. The light is poor, but you see a big, bird-like form approaching. At first you mistake it for an ostrich. It stands more than two metres (six feet) high. It strides on two long hind legs. But as it stalks closer you notice bizarre features that no ostriches possess. Instead of feathers, the beast has only tough, naked skin. Its long neck is tilted farther forward than an ostrich's, and balanced by a long, stiff tail held high up off the ground. Instead of wings, there are arms ending in clawed hands. This is no ostrich but an *Ornithomimus*, or 'bird mimic', one of a closely related group of big coelurosaurian dinosaurs.

A closer look at how their skeletons were built helps to explain the ostrich-like appearance. The bones are light and hollow, and the bird-like skull paper-thin in places, with a toothless, horny, bird-like beak instead of jaws with teeth. Moreover, the skull is set at a bird-like angle to the neck. The neck is long, but the gap between shoulder and hip girdle is small. Long foot bones allow the beast to run swiftly.

How these 'bird mimics' used their beaks and claws is uncertain. Possibly they tore open ants' nests with their hands, and then licked up the ants with a long, anteater-like tongue. Or they might have gathered molluscs by 'hand', and crushed them in their beaks. More likely they were omnivores, like modern ostriches. *Ornithomimus* could have shovelled sand away from dinosaurs' eggs, then pierced the shells and sucked the contents. It could also have eaten fruits and leaves, possibly de-husking fruit with its claws.

Pursued by enemies, these creatures very likely sprinted off at 80 km/hr (50 mph) – as fast as the ostriches they so closely resembled. No reptile would run that quickly. The energy required for such performances means that almost certainly *Ornithomimus* and other speedy coelurosaurs were warm blooded like the mammals.

Bird-hipped Bipeds

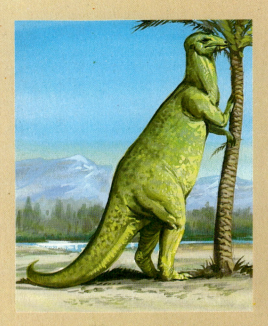  

Above: Three types of bird-hipped, bipedal dinosaur, showing their basic similarity of build. From Jurassic prototypes like Campto- saurus (left) came larger forms like Iguanodon (centre) and Corytho- saurus (right), one of the hadro- saurs, or 'duck-billed' dinosaurs.

Right: Camptosaurus skeletons in bipedal and quadrupedal poses. This dinosaur probably ambled along on all fours, but reared up on its hind legs to feed or travel quickly.

Spiky thumbs, crash-helmet skulls and bony crests make some of these herbivores among the strangest dinosaurs of all.

The 'lizard-hipped' sauropods were the largest-ever land animals. But these lumbering quadrupeds passed their peak in the Jurassic Period. Meanwhile, from the small 'bird-hipped' dinosaurs like *Fabrosaurus*, two other lines of bulky herbivores emerged, to reach their climax in Cretaceous times.

One line consisted of four-legged beasts. Members of the other group largely went around on hind legs only. This chapter is about these ornithischian ornithopod ('bird-footed') dinosaurs, to give the animals their scientific name.

A Bulky Herbivore
The first big ornithopod was *Camptosaurus*. Some individuals were no larger than a Shetland pony, others grew as long and heavy as the mightiest rhinoceros. *Camptosaurus* was built somewhat like a big flesh-eating dinosaur, but bulkier and heavier than most. Like those carnosaurs, it could stand up on its long, strong, hind limbs, balanced by its heavy tail, with its shortish fore-limbs held up off the ground.

But a close look at its design and way of life reveal the difference between this herbivore and the beasts that preyed upon it. First,

Camptosaurus had longer forelimbs than most carnosaurs. Instead of claws they bore flat nails and were designed for bearing weight rather than as arms with grasping hands.

Unlike *Allosaurus*, *Camptosaurus* probably went down on all fours when it was moving slowly. The curved shape of the creature's thigh bone suggests this posture and even gives the animal its name. *Camptosaurus* means 'bent reptile'. But *Camptosaurus* no doubt stood to reach food leaves high off the ground, and may have run on its hind legs when a big predator attacked. It certainly lacked the defences to fight off a hungry carnosaur. The hoof-like claws on its toes and fingers would have offered only weak resistance.

Camptosaurus's jaws were built for munching leaves, not tearing flesh. At the front end of its long, low skull was a horny beak that nipped leaves and twigs from *Camptosaurus*'s favourite plants. A long, snaky tongue rather like a giraffe's may have helped to haul this fodder inside his mouth. There, a row of leaflike cheek teeth ground the leaves to pulp fit for swallowing. While the teeth worked away at one batch of leaves, more batches waited

CLIMBER OR GROUND-DWELLER?

Hypsilophodon was a two-metre (six-foot) herbivore with long foot bones that suggest it was a swift runner. It ran with neck outstretched, balanced by a tapering, tendon-stiffened tail. Its big eyes and grasping toes led some experts to see *Hypsilophodon* as a climber and percher: a dinosaurian 'tree kangaroo'. Most experts now think it lived on the ground, outrunning its enemies.

in the roomy cheek pouches. Separate air passages prevented suffocation while *Camptosaurus* ate.

Iguanodon

By Cretaceous times the camptosaurs were fading out. But in the meantime they had given rise to even bigger bipeds. Best known of all is *Iguanodon* ('iguana tooth'), whose fossil bones and footprints crop up in many parts of southern England.

Iguanodon, at 8 metres (26 feet), was roughly twice as long as *Camptosaurus*. If it were still alive, this brute could have stood high enough to peer into an upstairs window. The body, carried on its huge hind legs, was as heavy as an elephant's.

Front legs relatively longer than those of *Camptosaurus* suggest that *Iguanodon*, too, could have gone down on all fours if it wanted.

Early in Cretaceous times, *Iguanodon* roamed lands as far apart as Africa and Spitsbergen – a chilly group of islands now well inside the Arctic Circle. In those balmy days its stamping grounds were warm, and ferns and ginkgoes (maidenhairs) and palm-like cycads flourished.

Iguanodon ate some or all of these kinds of plants, its horny beak snipping off fronds and twigs. Inside its mouth, whole rows of crowded teeth built up a battery of grinders that made *Iguanodon* even better than *Camptosaurus* at pulping

This Iguanodon can only save itself from Megalosaurus's fangs and claws by jabbing its spiky thumb into this carnosaur's eyes. Hypsilophodon and another Iguanodon (left) keep clear.

leaves. *Iguanodon* may have used its hands to prop itself up against the trees from which it fed, and possibly in mating. But the hands' special features were long thumbs which evolved as spikes. They were most likely *Iguanodon*'s main weapons. If savaged by a carnosaur, *Iguanodon* could have delivered painful stab wounds, especially by jabbing upwards at its attacker's eyes.

As *Iguanodon* munched its cow-like way across the countryside, it may have startled another, much smaller, biped. *Hypsilophodon* ('high-crested tooth') had a row of little teeth at the front end of the upper jaw, instead of just a horny pad like *Camptosaurus* and *Iguanodon*. But, like theirs, its cheek teeth were designed for grinding vegetation. *Hypsilophodon* must have been a timid herbivore. It was two metres (six feet) long and lighter than most men, but it may have run faster than any other dinosaur. A speedy getaway helped *Hypsilophodon* and its close kin to survive much longer than many of their giant cousins.

Boneheads
Some of the smallest but strangest of all bird-hipped bipeds were the bone-headed dinosaurs. They lived in Cretaceous North America, Asia and Europe. In most ways these dinosaurs looked unremarkable. They were built rather like light-weight camptosaurs, and they appear to have evolved from *Camptosaurus* via the turkey-sized *Yaverlandia*. *Yaverlandia* carried a long, stiff tail behind it, and two thickened areas of bone reinforced the top of its skull.

It was this tendency to grow a thickened skull that made the bone-

Right, top: The crack of skull on skull echoed around North American mountainsides as male boneheads jousted for mastery of the herd. Pachycephalosaurus's thick skull served as a crash helmet that protected it from brain damage when the beast used its head as a battering ram.

Right: Today, North American mountains still ring to the head-on clash between rival beasts, but now the contestants are mammals. Bighorn rams are browsers, dwelling in herds, each with its dominant male. This behaviour holds clues to how boneheaded dinosaurs must have lived long ago.

heads truly extraordinary. *Stegoceras* was a bonehead no taller than a man. Yet it housed its hen's-egg-sized brain under a skull roof five times thicker than a human cranium. A low bony frill jutted from the back of the skull.

Pachycephalosaurus ('thick-headed reptile') was a larger animal and even more bizarre. The skull was three times longer at the crown and almost five times thicker than *Stegoceras*'s. Sharp knobs projected from the back of the skull, and short bony spikes stuck up from the snout.

For years the boneheads' thick skulls puzzled scientists. Some thought they had been deformed by an overactive gland controlling growth. Others suggested that they had served as built-in crash helmets to protect the brain from damage in a fight with an enemy.

Yet boneheads had been harmless plant-eaters, browsing high on rocky mountainsides. Attacked by carnosaurs, the agile beasts would have run, not stood and fought. Their bony helmets could not have saved them from ferocious fangs and claws. Now, in fact, most experts believe that rival males used their heads as duelling weapons. Two males seeking to become the leader of a bonehead herd would have banged heads together until one animal submitted.

The 'Big Lizards'
No bird-hipped biped ever grew much larger than *Iguanodon*. But late in the Cretaceous Period lived

many bipeds of about the same size but of far stranger aspect. These were the hadrosaurs ('big lizards'), which thrived in all the northern continents.

In some ways hadrosaurs looked much like the iguanodonts. They averaged around 9 metres (30 feet) long, about the same as *Iguanodon*, but probably weighed considerably less. Like *Iguanodon*, they walked on strong hind legs equipped with three-toed feet. Their arms were well developed, but their hands lacked little fingers. Their thumbs were short and unspiky; the other fingers had hoof-like nails. A long, strong tail was flattened at the sides, rather more, even, than *Iguanodon*'s.

Dried, fossilized hadrosaur remains reveal that they had leathery skin studded with a pebbly mosaic of horny tubercles, larger on the back than on the belly. Some skin remains suggest that their fingers were webbed, but not all experts think so.

Webbed fingers and flattened tails would both hint that hadrosaurs were accomplished swimmers. Together with their flattened, duck-like jaws, these clues made many experts believe that these 'duck-billed dinosaurs' lived in water, munching soft waterweed, much as the sauropods had been held to do.

A horny, duck-like bill probably did sheath the duckbills' jaws. But while ducks are toothless, hadrosaurs possessed as many as 2000 grinding teeth. New ones constantly pushed upwards to replace the old

Two kinds of hadrosaur, or duck-billed dinosaur, browse on conifers and other Cretaceous vegetation. At right and centre are two Anatosaurus; at left, a Parasaurolophus. In the background, a third type, the high-crested Corythosaurus, wades in a shallow lake. These dinosaurs thrived in late Cretaceous North America. Most had a similar body build, but many kinds had head crests of different shapes. The hadrosaurs were peaceful herbivores. They lacked defensive weapons, but escaped danger by running or perhaps by swimming, sculling with their flattened tails.

Skulls shown here represent five major types of hadrosaur that sprang from a single ancestor, probably derived from Campto-saurus. Each of these skulls represents the end of a line of separate development. Experts have grouped hadrosaurs into two main divisions: Saurolophines, or solid-crested hadrosaurs, including Anatosaurus, Kritosaurus and Saurolophus; and Lambeosaurines, or hollow-crested hadrosaurs, like Corythosaurus and Parasauro-lophus.

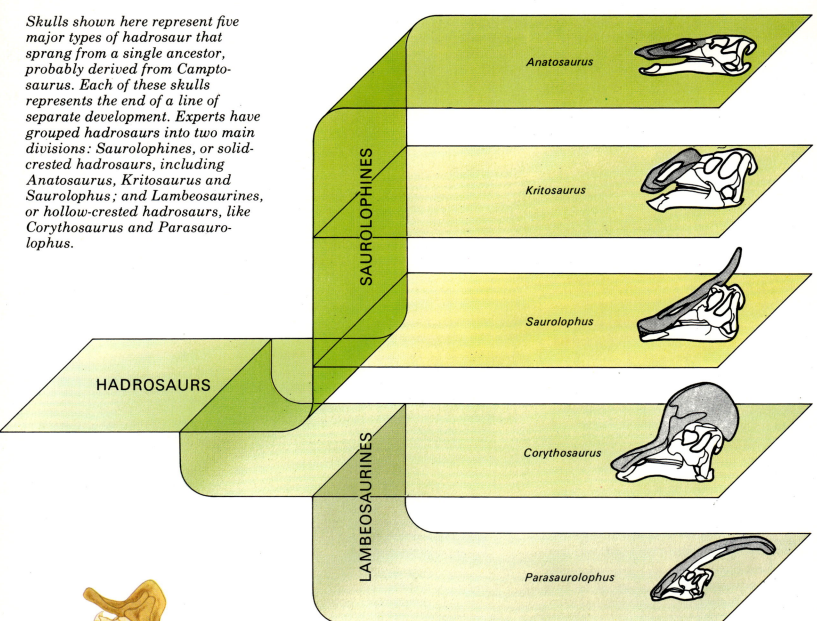

HADROSAURS

SAUROLOPHINES

Anatosaurus

Kritosaurus

Saurolophus

LAMBEOSAURINES

Corythosaurus

Parasaurolophus

Top to bottom: Skulls of Lambeo-saurus, Saurolophus and Parasaurolophus. Experts once thought the bony crests housed snorkels or scent detectors. Many now think they helped each hadrosaur to recognize its own kind.

ones as they wore down and fell out. This suggests a diet of hard, abrasive vegetation, not of soft water plants. Hadrosaurs were quite capable of champing on the tough-leaved flowering plants that were now advancing and driving out the soft-leaved vegetation on which many dinosaurs had lived in the past. In fact we have an actual sample of their diet: a jumbled mass of leaves, seeds, twigs and fruits preserved as fossils inside the skeleton of one hadrosaur. The chief ingredients were tough, needle-like leaves from a type of conifer. This makes it almost certain that the duckbills found their food on land, browsing on the woodland trees.

Those Curious Crests
What made the duck-billed dinosaurs especially remarkable was the way in which, in many, two frontal skull bones evolved into a crest jutting up from the head. These bones grew differently in each of several dozen species. No

cartoonist drawing imaginary monsters could invent a more bizarre array of heads than these.

From family resemblances between the skulls, some scientists have decided that hadrosaurs all fall into four main groups:

KRITOSAURS ('noble reptiles') get their name from a low nasal horn resembling a Roman nose.

SAUROLOPHINES ('reptile ridges') included unicorn-like species.

EDMONTOSAURS (so-called from fossils found in Canada's Edmonton rock formation) had flat heads with a nasal crest.

LAMBEOSAURINES included some hadrosaurs with a rounded 'helmet' and some with sweeping backswept 'horns'. Their name honours L. M. Lambe, a Canadian expert in the history of dinosaurs.

Why so many strange head shapes evolved baffled scientists. But they thought up some ingenious explanations. One suggested that the hollow crests whose passages connected with the nostrils had held stores of air to help their owners breathe while under water. Another notion was that long nasal passages must have made the creatures able to detect the faintest scent – an aid to finding food or fleeing enemies. Neither explanation rings true. The hollows would have held too little air for underwater breathing, and probably the nasal part that grew so large was not the 'smelling' area.

Another theory sounds much more likely. This holds that the different crests helped members of each species to recognize their kind. At first, perhaps, hadrosaurs had only low nasal horns, with which rivals butted one another. In some species, the horns grew longer and served to scare off rivals. Quite likely, inflatable 'balloons' could be blown up on openings on each side of a crest to draw attention to it. 'Balloons' and hollow crests might have served as resonators to amplify the bellowing of males defying rivals.

Below: Ornithopods (bird-hipped, bipedal dinosaurs) lived in every habitable continent. Iguanodonts roamed Europe, Africa and North America. Hypsilophodonts were represented there and in East Asia. The three northern continents became strongholds of the bone-heads and hadrosaurs.

The sclerotic ring, a circle of bones surrounding the eyeball, controlled eyeball size.

sclerotic ring

Above: A hadrosaur's skull, in this case that of Lambeosaurus, had a beak for cropping leaves and cheek teeth for mashing them.

A cutaway view of the skull (left) shows that the skull crest was hollowed out inside. When one male displayed his crest to another or to a female, he may also have bellowed. The hollow passage in his skull then acted as a resonator, intensifying the sound.

sites where ornithopod fossils have been found

Armoured Animals

Plated, horned and armoured dinosaurs resembled living tanks or armoured cars. At least some of them defied attack by even the fiercest flesh-eaters.

While some of the bird-hipped dinosaurs evolved as bipeds, others were four legged. These, too, had the horny beaks and hip girdles that showed that they were ornithischians, and, like their two-legged kin, they fed on plants. Unlike their biped relatives, however, most of the quadrupeds were slow movers. They stood their ground, and relied on built-in defences.

Some bore pairs of bony plates. Others were completely encased in living armour. Yet others sprouted horns. The last two types of protection proved the most effective. These big browsing creatures appear to have survived the fangs and claws of the greatest flesh-eaters. Only the disaster that overwhelmed the last dinosaurs eventually killed them.

All of the armoured quadrupeds probably stemmed from some small, inoffensive biped resembling fleet-footed *Hypsilophodon*. A chance fossil find in 1850 revealed remains of the first known plated dinosaur. About 190 million years ago, *Scelidosaurus* had roamed an ancient shore where the Dorset seaside town of Charmouth lies. The creature evidently had a low-slung, car-length body, with its high point at the hips. Broad feet and strong legs bore its considerable weight. The head was small, the jaws weak.

Scelidosaurus would have put up a poor fight against the big flesh-eating megalosaurs, but any creature that took a bite from its back risked snapping off its teeth. Low, bony plates arranged like stepping stones studded *Scelidosaurus*'s back from head to tail.

These jawbreakers gave the name stegosaurs ('plate reptiles') to the whole group that beasts like *Scelidosaurus* pioneered. Best known of all these dinosaurs is *Stegosaurus*, which roamed Jurassic North America in large numbers.

The Plated Giant
Stegosaurus was built along the same lines as *Scelidosaurus* but larger, and with greatly reinforced defences. It was nearly twice as long as *Scelidosaurus*, and stood room-high at the hips when it went on all fours. Scientists now think it also reared up on its hind legs to browse on trees.

Stegosaurus could bear most of its weight upon its hind limbs. Its long, straight thigh bones were like an elephant's, and the feet were broad, with big hoofed toes, backed by fatty cushions. Its massive tail, pressing down against the ground, helped to prop up and balance a *Stegosaurus* when rearing. Its teeth were few and feeble compared with those of the Cretaceous duck-billed dinosaurs, but they could cope with the soft, lush plants that abounded in Jurassic times.

Inside *Stegosaurus*'s tiny head was a brain no bigger than a walnut. A big hole at the base of the spinal cord was once thought to have held a 'sub-brain' – a knot of nerves co-ordinating movement of the hind limbs and the tail. But scientists

At 9 metres (30 feet) long, Stegosaurus was the largest of the plated dinosaurs, although less heavy than a hippopotamus. This small-brained herbivore browsed in North America and Europe in late Jurassic times. Stegosaurs lacked adequate protection against some carnosaurs, and they all became extinct well before the end of the Cretaceous Period.

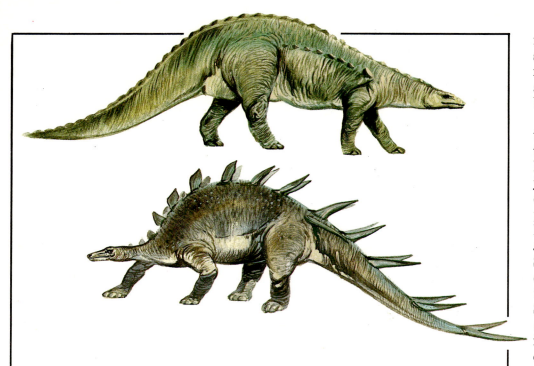

FROM BUMPS TO SPIKES

Perhaps the first plated dinosaur was *Scelidosaurus* (top), known only from a single, incomplete skeleton found in 1850 in England. Only low, triangular bumps on its back hinted at the big protective bony outgrowths of the later stegosaurs and ankylosaurs, descendants of this car-length quadruped.

Such spectacular defences included the double row of spikes on the back of *Kentrosaurus*, an African equivalent of *Stegosaurus*.

now believe the hole contained a special gland whose task was to make sure there was always an adequate supply of energy to the big back legs.

Stegosaurus's most striking feature was its armour. Two rows of triangular bony plates – some at least a metre (three feet) high – jutted from its back, and two pairs of bony spikes encased in horn projected sideways from the tail. Experts disagree about how *Stegosaurus* wore and used its armour. Some believe the plates protected only the backbone. Others think they were angled to guard the flanks. Studies of the tail suggest that *Stegosaurus* could not have swung it sideways as a club. Maybe inadequate defence was why the stegosaurs died out before Cretaceous times got under way, though they had persisted for 50 million years.

Tank-like Monsters

There now emerged a group of dinosaurs with a much more complete and seemingly effective covering of

Ankylosaurus swings its massive, club-like tail to ward off an attack by Gorgosaurus. Only by overturning it can the flesh-eater disarm and kill this low-slung, tank-like dinosaur.

armour plating. These squat, low, heavy-bodied beasts are named ankylosaurs ('rounded reptiles') from the curved shapes of their ribs. They probably shared a common ancestor with plated dinosaurs; some indeed resembled the early plated varieties.

One of the first-known ankylosaurs was *Polacanthus*, which lived in Europe before the stegosaurs became extinct. Fossil bones show a low, flattened dinosaur, longer than *Scelidosaurus*, but also highest at the hips. It had a heavy tail, powerful limbs, and a small head. A double row of tall, spiky cones guarded the back of the neck and front part of the back. A bony corset studded with small bosses shielded *Polacanthus*'s hips. Two rows of triangular bony plates protected the tail. The creature looked somewhat like a gigantic armadillo.

Southern England was also home to *Acantopholis*, another early type of ankylosaur. *Acantopholis* was about as long as *Polacanthus*, but far less spiky. Instead, flattish bony plates covered the back and tail. Small spines may have bristled from the shoulders.

The tendency towards long, low, heavy, armoured shapes grew strongest among some dinosaurs that lived in late Cretaceous times. *Euoplocephalus* (the correct name for what was once called *Ankylosaurus*) was a tank-like monster only half as long as *Stegosaurus*, but twice as heavy. Rows of flattish plates guarded the top of its head and the entire top and sides of its neck, back and tail. Great bony bosses overlapped the eyes and nostrils of its low, triangular skull. But the only weapon of attack was a tail tip thickened like a bony club.

Even heavier and perhaps yet more impregnable, was *Scolosaurus* ('thorn reptile'). Bony plates and tough skin protected its upper parts; and neck, back and flanks bore rows of thick, blunt, bony cones sheathed by sharp horny spikes. Even the upper arm was shielded in this way. But the biggest spikes of all were two that jutted from the end of the thick, heavy, bony tail. Perhaps

Scolosaurus (left) was arguably even better defended than Ankylosaurus. Besides the bony plates and horny spikes that sheathed the back and flanks, Scolosaurus had spikes that jutted from its tail and upper forelegs. An astonishingly lifelike fossil of its carapace (below) gives a clear idea of how the back was armoured. Scolosaurus lived in late Cretaceous North America. It ate low-growing plants but not grasses – these had not evolved in Mesozoic times.

Scolosaurus waved this like a living mace. But the tail may have been too clumsy to be wielded accurately. Slow-moving *Scolosaurus* must have resembled a gigantic spiky tortoise as it shuffled along.

Of all ankylosaurs, *Palaeoscincus* posed the thorniest problem for would-be predators. Flat, bony plates encased its back, while a row of formidable spikes jutting outwards from the sides deterred a flank attack.

An ankylosaur's only soft, unarmoured surface was its belly. Usually this did not matter, for the belly lay too near the ground to be attacked. The real danger would have come from any carno-

Below: Psittacosaurus ('parrot reptile') was ancestral to the horned dinosaur – the last group to evolve. Its skeleton shows that Psittacosaurus was the length of a man and capable of running semi-upright. The powerful jaws and 'parrot's beak' were probably designed for biting off and crushing tough-leaved vegetation. Early on in the Cretaceous Period such plants were emerging in east-central Asia where it lived.

Opposite page: Rich finds of fossil eggs and adult animals help us to reconstruct this scene in the life of Protoceratops, a two-metre (six-foot) long precursor of the great horned dinosaurs. Baby Protoceratops burst forth from eggs laid by their mothers in the sand and hatched by the sun's heat. Meanwhile the adults use their beak-like jaws to slice off mouthfuls of tough palm fronds.

saurs big, strong, bold and brainy enough to overturn the animal. The fact that all ankylosaur fossils have been discovered upside down suggests this. But this death position could also result from drowning. A drowned ankylosaur would have floated with its belly uppermost. Then, lodged upon a mudbank, it would eventually have been covered with layers of sediment.

The rather few fossil finds of ankylosaurs that have been made suggest that they were never plentiful. Far more numerous were some of the horned dinosaurs that also came upon the late Cretaceous scene. So many of their fossil skeletons survive that we have a pretty clear idea just how this line of dino-

saurs began and branched out, and how they fought, fed and bred.

Horned Beasts

The forefather of all horned dinosaurs was a creature like *Psittacosaurus* ('parrot reptile'). This two-legged dinosaur, no longer than a man, lived in China and Mongolia early in the Cretaceous Period. It may have walked on all fours. But strong hind legs, much longer than its front legs, suggest that *Psittacosaurus* could have walked or run half upright, balanced by its long, sturdy tail. Either way, it was not well designed for sprinting.

What made *Psittacosaurus* special was its deep skull, ending in the 'parrot beak' that gives this dinosaur its name. Scientists suspect this beak evolved to help the animal chop off the new, tough-leaved flowering plants that were then appearing.

It remains a puzzle how small, slow-moving, and defenceless beasts like this survived long enough to father the horned dinosaurs. But somehow they did. We even have the fossil of a 'half-way' animal that helps to bridge the gap between psittacosaurine dinosaurs and the true ceratopsians ('horned faces'). Little *Leptoceratops* lived when these giants were already well established. But its old-fashioned build shows the kind of creature that their ancestors may well have been. *Leptoceratops* was about the same size as *Psittacosaurus* and about as heavy as a man. It may have run erect but could have walked on all four legs. The skull was deep and beaked, and had a flat crest thrust back above the neck.

In *Protoceratops* ('first horned face') this crest formed a big shield covering the neck and shoulders. This bony frill helped to guard nerves, sinews and blood vessels in the neck. But its main job was providing anchorage for powerful muscles. Strong jaw muscles helped *Protoceratops* bite on tough-leaved plants, and strong neck muscles helped support its heavy jaws and head, for its head was nearly three-quarters as long as its back.

So much is plain from the many fossils of this animal found in Mongolia during and since the 1920s. But the most exciting finds were the fossil eggs discovered with these dinosaurs. In 1923 came the first evidence of how dinosaurs actually reproduced their own kind.

The female *Protoceratops* had first

scooped out a hollow in warm sand, and then deposited her clutch of eggs. Each egg was elongated, about 20 cm (8 inches) long, and possibly protected by a leathery jacket like that of lizards' eggs. The mother laid her eggs in a kind of horizontal spiral, the narrower end of each egg facing the inside of the ring. Sometimes one circle was laid above another, and some scientists suggest that two or more females may have laid in the same nest. Once a clutch was complete, the mother heaped sand above the eggs and left them in the sun to hatch. Sometimes things went wrong. Fossils have been found of embryos that died only half developed, and of young that died shortly after hatching. No other fossil finds tell us so much about the ways in which a dinosaur began its life.

Horns and Frills

But *Protoceratops* was small and insignificant compared with what came later. From this prototype, a mere two metres (six feet) long, evolved ceratopsians with longer horns and frills, and far bigger bodies. There were several lines and several branches, each with its own frill and horn design.

One otherwise unknown line threw up *Pachyrhinosaurus* ('thick-nose reptile'), a hornless beast with thick bone shielding the upper front part of its head. This ceratopsian may have fought duels in the fashion of the boneheads. Another curiosity was *Styracosaurus* ('spiny reptile'), with a long, nasal horn and a frill edged with spikes.

Two lines of ceratopsians are better known. One line had three stout horns, and a long, back-swept, bony frill. Among the first of these long-frilled ceratopsians was *Chasmosaurus*, which had big frill openings, a small nasal horn and two big horns that jutted from its brows. Such dinosaurs gave rise to *Pentaceratops* ('five-horned face'), a bigger beast with larger horns and an extra pair of hornlike bony knobs projecting from the cheeks. Later still came *Torosaurus* with enormous

sites where plated, horned, or
armoured dinosaur fossils have been found

*Below: Triceratops drives off
Tyrannosaurus in this scene from
late Cretaceous North America.
Horned dinosaurs were peaceful
browsers but formidable in defence.
Measuring 11 metres (36 feet) and
weighing 8·5 tonnes, Triceratops
was the most massive of them all,
dwarfing today's rhinoceroses.*

*Above: Plated dinosaurs inhabited
Jurassic North America, Europe,
Africa and Asia. These continents
and South America were also home
to the armoured dinosaurs of
Cretaceous times. But the late
Cretaceous horned dinosaurs lived
only in East Asia and western
North America.*

brow horns and a frill that reached
beyond the shoulders.

Another line, of short-frilled ceratopsians, ended with *Triceratops*
('three-horned face'), the last and
largest of all ceratopsians. Among
the dinosaurs only the giant sauropods outranked this monster in size.
Triceratops measured 11 metres (36
feet) long and heavier than a bull
elephant. Its head was one quarter
the length of its whole body. Its
nasal horn was short, but a pair of
horns almost a metre (three feet)
long projected from the brows. Even
Tyrannosaurus would have fled from
the lowered, spiky head of a charg-
ing *Triceratops*. But sometimes the
great rhinoceros-like dinosaur un-
doubtedly clashed head-on with an
enemy. Proof of such battles lies in
old, healed fractures of the horns,
jaws and neck-frill found in some of
the *Triceratops* fossils from North
America.

Triceratops probably passed its
days mostly in quietly browsing
herds. Even the toughest vegetation
was no problem for its great beak, or
for the shearing action of its sharp
teeth worked by jaw muscles more
than a metre (three feet) long. Palm
and cycad fronds may have been its
chief fodder, although *Triceratops*
continued to flourish when cool-
climate, deciduous plants had begun to take their place.

Adventurers in Air and Water

Bottom: This fossil Rhamphorhynchus ('prow beak') was fairly typical of early pterosaurs. The length of a magpie, it had a long, narrow head with huge eye sockets. Its teeth projected forward, probably to help the creature spear fish. The long tail had a broad, upright, stiffened skin tip serving as a rudder. An enormously long fourth finger supported each wing of skin, from which projected three more fingers armed with claws.

dwarfed the largest eagle. All had bodies made for flight in most, if not all, of the ways we have outlined. Their long arm bones and even longer fourth-finger bones formed the leading edges for tapering wings of skin whose rear edges swept back to join the hind legs.

The skeleton or 'airframe' was largely built of strong, but slim and strawlike, hollow bones. These lightweight tubes appear to have held air as do the hollow bones of birds.

But many pterosaurs evidently lacked the necessary muscle power for flapping flight. Their breast bones supported feeble flight muscles and their wings were shaped for gliding on the updraughts of air that rise from hot land or up cliffs.

The pterosaurs' fossil skulls have big eye sockets and brain cavities,

From land-bound reptiles evolved winged and flippered creatures that between them ruled the skies and seas.

Dinosaurs controlled the land in Mesozoic times. But other types of backboned animal won mastery in air and water.

The air offered many benefits. Airborne animals could easily escape most predators. They could rear their young high on crags or in trees out of reach of harm. By catching insects or swooping down on fish they could tap a new supply of food.

But no animal can fly without the right equipment. To resist gravity, the body must be light and winged. Controlled flight calls for keen sight, precise muscular co-ordination and a delicate sense of balance. And such active animals may have had to be warm blooded.

Winged Reptiles
It took time to evolve all these ingredients. By late Triassic times, lizard-like reptiles with a web of skin between their limbs and body were gliding down from rocks or trees. By Jurassic times such ancestors had given rise to pterosaurs ('winged reptiles'). Some were sparrow-sized, others would have

Three pterosaurs that lived at different times during the Mesozoic Era. Dimorphodon (left) had a blunt, short head armed with teeth, a long tail, and wings rather like a bat's, but more flimsily supported. It lived in early Jurassic times. Rhamphorhynchus (right) came later. One of the last and largest pterosaurs was the great glider Pteranodon (centre). A bony crest balanced the weight of its big, toothless beak.

showing they were keen eyed and capable of delicate manoeuvring. They could have snatched moving prey from air or water in their beaklike jaws as they flew or glided.

On land, though, their short legs made them almost helpless. They may have shuffled along on their knuckles, or merely roosted upside down like bats. Three forward-pointing fingers on each wing might have helped them climb up trees and rocks.

Furry Flyers
Two main groups of pterosaurs evolved. First came the rhampho-

Above (left to right): The wings of a pterosaur, bird and bat. Pterosaur wings were webs of skin supported largely by one finger. They were less capable of flapping flight than birds' or bats' wings, which are reinforced by several fingers. Pterosaurs' wings were also more likely to be torn irreparably.

A colony of Pteranodon fishes and feeds its young by sea cliffs where the state of Kansas lies today. These giant, weak-winged gliders skimmed the waves to snatch up fish in their beaks, storing them in a capacious throat pouch like a pelican's. Parents disgorge their catch to their young, safely crouched on cliff ledges out of reach of predatory dinosaurs. Pteranodon may also have roosted, bat-like, hanging upside down from rocks. Their neighbours on the cliff are the gull-sized Ichthyornis. Below, closer to the sea, are several Hesperornis, birds that, like penguins, could not fly.

rhynchoids ('prow beaks'). Their fairly short, broad wings remind us of crows rather than albatrosses: they may have flapped instead of gliding. They also had long tails that served as rudders, and beak-like jaws bristling with teeth.

Fossil finds from the Jurassic Period suggest that possibly these pterosaurs had fur. *Sordes pilosus* ('hairy devil') certainly had such a body covering because, in 1971, an entire specimen, complete with fur, was found in the Soviet Union. By helping to stop body heat leaking away, this insulating layer would keep in more energy for flight.

The second major group of pterosaurs appeared late in the Jurassic Period (at the same time as the birds, whose origins we look at in another chapter). These were the pterodactyloids ('winged fingers'), some much bigger than the largest rhamphorhynchoid pterosaurs.

The early type called *Pterodactylus* included species no larger

than a sparrow. These small aeronauts were also designed to carry less weight. The long steering tail had shrunk to a mere stub. Some wing bones had grown relatively longer, and a horny beak had begun to take the place of toothed jaws.

Another pterodactyloid was *Dsungaripterus*, from early Cretaceous times. This animal had jaws with spiky tips, probably designed for spearing fish.

New types of larger pterodactyloids appeared during the Cretaceous Period. Until the 1970s *Pteranodon* ('winged and toothless') was the largest pterosaur to be discovered. *Pteranodon*'s wingspread would have spanned over 7 metres (24 feet); but its body was no larger than a turkey's. The same area of manmade glider wing must support four times the load borne by *Pteranodon*'s wings. *Pteranodon* relied on winds to get it airborne; its muscles lacked the power for flapping flight.

Dwarfing even this gigantic glider

71

was a pterosaur discovered in the early 1970s. *Quetzalcoatlus* ('feathered serpent') had twice the wingspan of *Pteranodon*. In theory no such creature could have got off the ground. Yet *Quetzalcoatlus* evidently soared and fed on carrion like modern vultures, on an inland plain where Texas stands today.

Reptiles take to the Sea

All reptiles breathe air. But early in the Age of Dinosaurs, some turned increasingly to water for their food supply. The seas offered these enterprising animals a fish and shellfish harvest. Some found all the food they wanted at the sea's edge. Others learned to swim and dive for prey. Such reptiles were to give rise to sea beasts as agile as any fish or whale.

However, they all still had to come up for air, and some no doubt pulled themselves ashore to lay eggs, or to give birth, as seals do now. Others would have beached themselves to bask. *Tanystropheus* was arguably the most astonishing of all such animals. This close relative of the lizards lived in and by the sea in Europe during middle Triassic times. The reptile was longer than three men laid end to end. But three-quarters of it consisted of a long, tubular neck, supported by

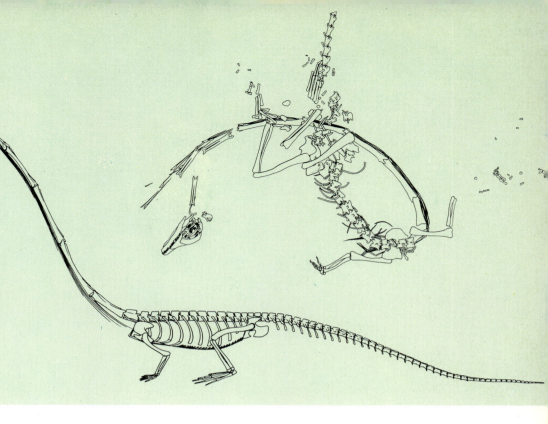

LONG-NECKED LIZARD

Even the jumble of fossil bones of *Tanystropheus* reveals the grotesquely long, stiff neck that once projected from the body. Earlier finds of partial skeletons had led scholars to think that they had found bits of two entirely different animals. The reconstructed skeleton shows clearly the 11 vertebrae that made up this creature's neck.

only 11 vertebrae. More like a stiff rod than a flexible hosepipe, it is hard to see what this neck was for. Maybe it helped its owner fish without getting its feet wet. *Tanystropheus* could have stood on shore and plunged its small head under water to seize fish and molluscs. But its long neck would have made *Tanystropheus* vulnerable to many predators. Not surprisingly, the creature did not survive into the Jurassic Period.

Placodus's skull (right) had peg-like front teeth to uproot shellfish, and flat back teeth to crush them.

Below: Reptilian aquanauts seek food from the sea in this Triassic scene. Tanystropheus could have fished from the shore by plunging its long neck under water. Placodus foraged for shellfish on the sea bed. Nothosaurs caught fish in their sharp teeth.

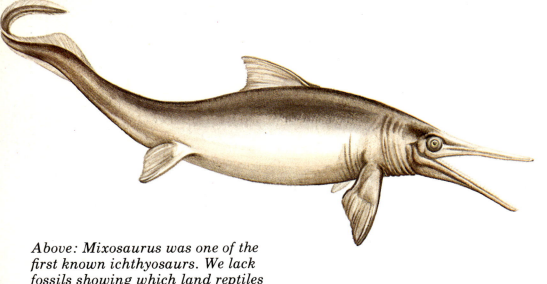

Above: Mixosaurus was one of the first known ichthyosaurs. We lack fossils showing which land reptiles these fish-like creatures came from.

Fossil bones and body outline (top) enable artists to reconstruct Ichthyosaurus (above).

in long, sharp teeth designed to stop their slippery catch escaping.

While nothosaurs pounced on free-swimming prey, placodonts were grubbing for shellfish on the sea bed below. Their strange teeth were well adapted for this purpose. Placodonts were stubbier, short-bodied versions of the nothosaurs. Bony lumps provided some sort of protection for their bodies.

'Fish Lizards'

A swimming placodont or nothosaur, when compared with *Ichthyosaurus* ('fish lizard'), would have seemed like a propeller-driven plane outraced by *Concorde*. It is probable

Nothosaurs and placodonts were two more Triassic reptile curiosities. Nothosaur fossils turn up in places as far apart as England and Japan. No other sea-going reptiles were so plentiful. Ranging up to 6 metres (20 feet) long, they resembled huge lizards. They had long, slim snouts and necks, and tails flattened at the sides to help them swim. Their feet were probably webbed, but their legs were long enough to allow them to walk easily on land. Fossils show that their young were born or hatched on beaches and in caves. Nothosaurs would have spent most days hunting fish, which they seized

that no reptile ever swam so fast or gracefully as this creature, which so strikingly resembled a modern dolphin.

Like the dolphin, ichthyosaurs had sacrificed legs for flippers and evolved a streamlined, 'neckless' body. A fish-like backbone enabled them to swim with long, arching movements. With powerful thrusts of its big, upright tailfin, the ichthyosaur cut through water more smoothly than a high-speed submarine. A tall, fish-like fin projecting upward from its back helped to keep the creature upright. Ichthyosaurs braked and steered with the help of broad flippers projecting from their sides. Sharp teeth in their tapered snouts crunched up fish, ammonites and other prey, as fossil stomach contents show. Ichthyosaurs' appetites no doubt matched their size—3 to 10 metres (9 to 33 feet) in length.

So well adapted were these 'fish reptiles' for a water life that they could not return to land to lay eggs. Instead, their young were born in water, although they must have

Above: A fossil Ichthyosaurus thought to be giving birth to young. Other fossil skeletons have been found with as many as four small skeletons inside them.

Below: A pliosaur, or short-necked plesiosaur, attacks a long-necked plesiosaur. Pliosaurs swam powerfully and must have set upon their prey somewhat as a killer whale does today.

Prehistoric giants of land and water meet in mortal combat at the river's edge. Phobosuchus ('horror crocodile') attacks a hadrosaur that has ventured down to take a drink. This colossal crocodile of late Cretaceous times was evidently built to prey on dinosaurs. It had a ferociously fanged skull the length of a man. The silhouettes (inset) show that the longest modern crocodile is dwarfed beside Phobosuchus's powerful 15-metre (50-foot) body.

started breathing air at once, as baby whales do.

Powerful Paddles

Ichthyosaurs lived in all three periods of Mesozoic time, but the nothosaurs and placodonts did not survive into the Jurassic Period. By then, however, the nothosaurs had launched a line of long-lived descendants. These new sea reptiles were the plesiosaurs, or 'near lizards'. Most plesiosaurs were longer and stronger than most nothosaurs. Their tails were too short to help them scull along. Instead they rowed with limbs like powerful paddles. These pressed back flat against the water to thrust the body forward, then swept forward, edge on to the water, ready for the next stroke. To veer left or right, a plesiosaur simply backed water with both paddles on one side. In this way the big sea monsters manoeuvred their great flat-bellied bodies with

surprising skill for their size.

There were two sorts of plesiosaur. One group had longish paddles, a short neck and a big head with strong jaws. The other group had short paddles, and a long neck with a small head. 'A snake threaded through a turtle' is how one writer described the second group. Such beasts probably swam rather slowly but caught fish with quick stabs of their long, flexible necks. More than 70 neck vertebrae took up over half the total length of *Elasmosaurus* ('ribbon reptile'). *Elasmosaurus* was 12 metres (40 feet) long and lived in late Cretaceous times.

Such long-necked fish-eaters would have proved no match for their biggest short-necked relatives. Among the largest and most powerful of these so-called pliosaurs was *Kronosaurus*. This 17-metre-long (56-foot) predator is known from fossils in Australia. Its head measured 4 metres (13 feet). Long-necked plesiosaurs and ichthyosaurs may well have fallen victim to this monster.

The Familiar Crocodiles

No aquatic reptiles so far mentioned outlived the Mesozoic Era. But the Age of Dinosaurs also saw the rise of swimming reptiles with a more familiar aspect.

The largest among these beasts were the crocodilians. Crocodilians arose from small, short-headed, Triassic forebears such as *Protosuchus*. By Jurassic times sea-going crocodilians included *Teleosaurus*, whose long, slim, sharp-toothed jaws were shaped for seizing fish. Jurassic seas also held *Geosaurus* – a crocodile with seal-like flippers and a tail fin rather like an ichthyosaur's.

But the biggest crocodiles of all haunted inland lakes and rivers. *Phobosuchus* – the biggest crocodilian that ever lived – had a head longer than *Tyrannosaurus*'s, about 2 metres (6 feet) in length. It may well have preyed on dinosaurs in late Cretaceous North America.

Early on in the Cretaceous Period some monitor-like lizards also took to water. By late Cretaceous times they had given rise to mosasaurs – giant, sea-going lizards 15 metres (48 feet) long. Mosasaurs had short, flipper-like limbs and webbed toes. Their tails were deep and flattened at the sides. These long-bodied creatures swam with snaky undulations. Jaws with an elastic gape enabled them to gulp food in huge mouthfuls. Mosasaur tooth-marks found on fossil ammonites show that even big, shell-protected molluscs were not safe from the sea lizards.

Aquatic turtles, too, evolved and took on shapes similar to those alive today. But their ancestors were land tortoises which lived on land in late Triassic times. Tank-like beasts such as *Proganochelys* sacrificed mobility to skulk within the safety of a heavy, bony 'overcoat'. Later on in Mesozoic time, some of its descendants took to water, where armour plating proved more hindrance than help. Marine turtles gained mobility by developing a lightweight shell, and limbs designed as long, strong flippers. Late Cretaceous seas were home to creatures like *Archelon*, at 4 metres (13 feet) long, the largest turtle of all time. No living turtles are as big as that, but they are built on much the same lines. Of the other Mesozoic reptiles that took up life in water, only the crocodilians survive.

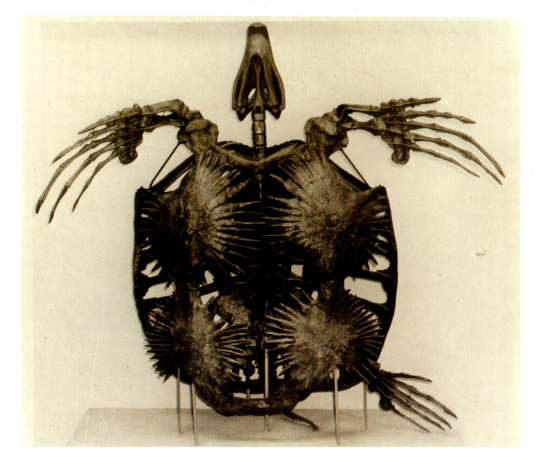

Above: The heavily armoured skeleton of Archelon, the largest sea turtle ever known. Its shell was hard enough to resist all but the most powerful teeth.

Below: Today, warm seas and remote islands still provide a natural habitat for some of the large turtles, such as this loggerhead from the Red Sea.

Vanishing Dinosaurs

About 65 million years ago, the last dinosaur lay dead. What killed the dinosaurs remains one of the great unsolved mysteries of the prehistoric past.

Dinosaurs were among the most durable and thus successful of all land animals. Compared with their 140 million-year reign, Man's time on Earth is just an eye-blink.

Yet as Cretaceous time advanced, there were signs that their lengthy rule was ending. Some dinosaurs, of course, had already become extinct earlier in the Mesozoic Era. But they had left behind descendants that carried on the line. By very late in the Cretaceous Period, duckbilled, horned and armoured dinosaurs remained abundant, but the numbers of their species had slumped by more than half. Then some unknown blow struck down the rest.

A 'Sudden' End

Disaster fell relatively swiftly. A change in the record of the rocks tells the story. One layer is rich in dinosaur remains, the next has none. One moment (geologically speaking) horned dinosaurs, huge sauropods and fierce tyrannosaurs were still striding the earth; the next instant all had gone for ever. We know that this happened about 65 million years ago.

The same doom that hit the dinosaurs seems to have struck down a host of other animals. Land, sea and air were all affected. Late Cretaceous times saw those master gliders the pterosaurs and those superb

Small mammals plunder a clutch of Alamosaurus eggs, while the dinosaur that laid them is distracted by a prowling Tyrannosaurus. Some people suggest that thieving mammals with a taste for egg wiped out the whole great tribe of dinosaurs. Others argue that Mesozoic mammals were too small and few to have achieved this, and even if they could, why did they wait until the very end of the Cretaceous Period?

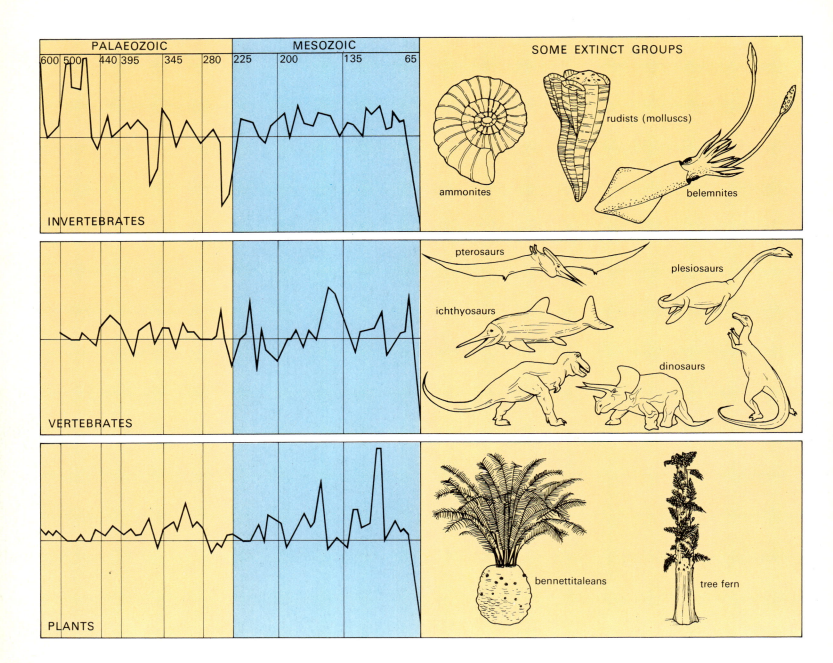

A graph of the rise and fall of species during the Palaeozoic and Mesozoic Eras shows the dramatic number of extinctions at the end of the Mesozoic. The extinction of the dinosaurs as a group accounts for the sharp drop among the vertebrates, but there were also extinctions on a relatively large scale among the invertebrates and in the plant world.

swimmers the ichthyosaurs wiped out. When the final mass extinction of the dinosaurs occurred, the plesiosaurs and mosasaurs – last of the big sea-going reptiles apart from certain crocodiles – went too. And with them disappeared a wealth of small marine invertebrates, including ammonites: creatures much older even than the dinosaurs.

What killed the dinosaurs and the ancient flying and sea-going reptiles remains one of the great puzzles of the past. Many efforts have been made to solve it. All theories are really guesses – but some are much wilder and more improbable than others.

A Wave of Theories

Perhaps the zaniest occur among a group of notions suggesting that in some way or another the dinosaurs destroyed themselves. When mountains rose and climates cooled late in Cretaceous times, the small-brained brutes were just too stupid to adapt themselves to changed

conditions, runs one argument.

Another has it that some were so incompetently built that slipped discs immobilized them. Thick skulls produced by bony overgrowth persuaded other theorists that the boneheads and perhaps other groups suffered glandular defects that also sterilized them. The toothlessness of some bird-like dinosaurs, and the fancy helmets, spikes and armour-plating of many of the last dinosaurs, convinced some scientists that these must have been far too specialized to cope with any major change to their surroundings. These bizarre body structures were taken to be signs that the last dinosaurs all suffered from a kind of collective old age.

But these theories ignore the fact that the dinosaurs were not monstrosities; they were built to cope effectively with the world they lived in. Moreover, the bird-like dinosaurs, at least, were relatively brainy. Most of these theories, then, are no more convincing than the idea that the flesh-eaters killed all the plant-eaters and simply died of famine.

Disease or Poison?

That the dinosaurs did not destroy themselves, but were the victims of disease, was yet another theory. This held that deadly germs passed from beast to beast swept the world clean of dinosaurs like some even more devastating version of the plague that ravaged Europe and Asia in the Middle Ages. But this theory, too, ignores the mass death of organisms unrelated to the dinosaurs. No known germ could kill so many kinds of animal.

Small mammals with an appetite for dinosaur eggs are sometimes blamed for the final disaster. No doubt the furtive, furry mammals of those days did feast upon such banquets when they could. The mammals, however, were active throughout the Mesozoic Era – why should they suddenly pose such a threat to the dinosaurs? And, too, modern Nile crocodiles persist, although their eggs are often thieved by lizards.

Passing from animals to plants, we find a fresh list of suspects. The flowering plants, busy ousting older kinds during the Cretaceous Period, are blamed for flavours the dinosaurs disliked and poisons that proved lethal. It is true enough that distasteful or noxious substances help many plants wage passive war

Clouds of hot volcanic ash, released in sudden, dramatic upheavals of the earth's crust, form the basis for one theory which attempts to explain the extinction of the dinosaurs. This explanation seems unlikely, for the simple reason that such isolated disasters could not have wiped out species all over the Cretaceous world.

Opposite page: Autumn in late Cretaceous North America. Gone is the lush evergreen vegetation on which herbivorous dinosaurs once browsed. Many of the trees that grow instead now shed their leaves as winter approaches. Intensifying cold and lack of food may have put paid to this Styracosaurus and all other dinosaurs living in this last phase of the Mesozoic Era.

Fossils like that of Struthiomimus, a relative of Ornithomimus, have been found with the neck thrown back, as though the creature had died of poisoning. This might appear to suggest that the dinosaurs were wiped out by some toxic substance in their food. In reality, however, this posture is caused by the shrinking of the animal's neck ligaments after death.

against beasts that otherwise would eat them. Dinosaurs may have avoided bitter-flavoured flowering plants, but it seems unlikely that they ate enough alkaloid-rich leaves to die from poisoning. Indeed, the horned and duck-billed dinosaurs had beaks seemingly designed to help them cope with many of the tough-leaved flowering plants that came to dominate the lands they lived in.

People have found fossil ostrich-like dinosaurs with their heads thrown back in the characteristic pose of a bird poisoned by strychnine. This pose, however, shows only that their neck ligaments shrank after death, not that the creatures had been poisoned.

Natural Disasters

None of these theories explains why the pterosaurs and ichthyosaurs died out at the same time as the dinosaurs. Casting the net wider, some people have speculated that disaster rained down on the earth from outer space. Meteorites or comets, they say, damaged the make-up or pressure of the very air the creatures breathed. Or a distant star exploded, showering earth with cosmic rays that deformed the creatures' unborn young.

Other theorists look nearer home for the source of the calamity. They blame floods; poisoned gases thrown off by volcanoes; earthquakes and other violent activities in the earth's

crust that may have baked or chilled the lands and seas.

The likeliest explanation seems to be some sort of sweeping climatic change. By late Cretaceous times, large land areas once in the tropics had drifted into colder zones. Meanwhile clashing continents had thrown up mountain ranges, sea areas were redistributed and ocean levels fell. These changes all helped to bring cold winters to places where such seasons had been hitherto unknown.

On land, broad-leafed trees that shed their foliage in winter increasingly replaced the soft, lush ferns and cycads. Autumn leaf-fall foretold hungry months ahead for the plant-eating dinosaurs. Small, cold-blooded beasts like snakes and lizards – even alligators – burrowed in the ground and hibernated. Warm-blooded birds and mammals stayed active, insulated from the cold by feathers or fur.

The dinosaurs found no escape from the cooling climate. Warm blooded though they very probably were, they lacked any covering to stop heat leaking from their naked hides. Uninsulated from the cold, and too big to burrow into the earth, the giants slowed down, grew numb, then perished where they stood or fell.

Much of this, of course, is surmise, but no other theory so convincingly explains what could have brought the Age of Reptiles to its end.

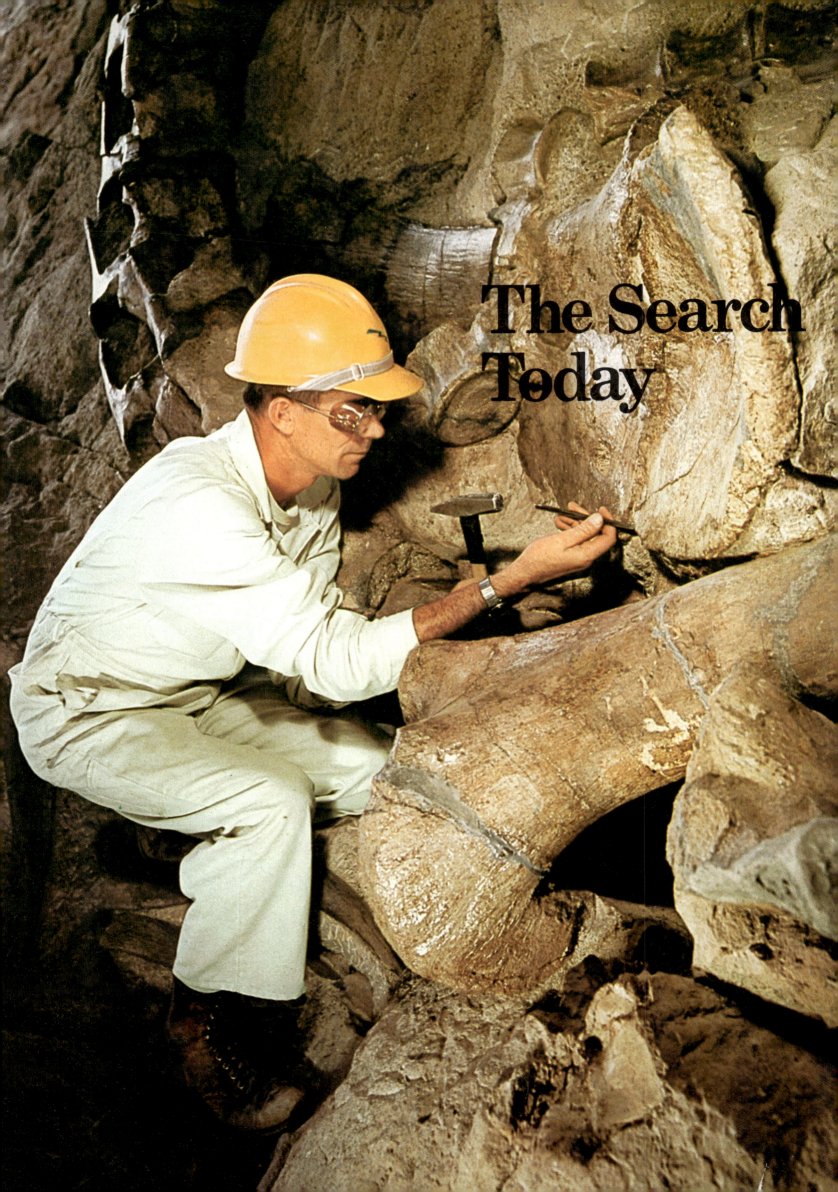

The Search Today

Fossil dinosaur bones lie in rock like bits of a lost jigsaw puzzle. To glimpse the whole picture, Man must find and match the many pieces.

Modern dinosaur hunters are more sophisticated than the Wild West pick-and-shovel gangs of Cope and Marsh, but much of their procedure is the same. The first step is to find a likely hunting ground – a place where there are outcrops of rock formed during the Mesozoic Era. Badlands, where soil erosion has stripped away the top-soil and revealed large tracts of weathered rock, are the most likely places for such finds. The practised hunter trudges slowly with his eyes on the ground, scanning the gullies and the bases of cliffs where fossils washed out from above are likely to collect.

Most people, seeing a fossil in such a setting, would think it just another bit of rock. But the keen eye of the trained hunter detects some sign of texture that sets the piece apart from any ordinary stone: the bone's spongy-looking inner surface, perhaps, or the smooth gleam of its outer surface.

Digging Out Fossils

Finding a fossil fragment is only the beginning. Next comes the search for the rock layer from which gravity and rain have washed the fossil. The lucky hunter may discover whole skeletons embedded in this layer. Even greater luck is needed to get them out intact. Too often, they lie half way up an almost sheer cliff face.

Provided he can reach it, the hunter makes a trial dig around the skeleton to find out how big it is and what sort of condition it is in. Sometimes too much of the creature has gone to make a complete excavation worth while.

Even if a dig is possible, the task is daunting. It may require a whole team of fossil hunters, with special machinery and tools.

Freeing a fossil dinosaur may mean first bulldozing or blowing up huge quantities of rock before the team can set to work by hand. Each digger may start by using pick and shovel for the rough preliminary work. Then he probes more carefully: chipping rock away with hammers and chisels, gouging with

awls or builder's trowels, or wire-brushing earth and stones away. Removing the bones intact is slow, demanding work. One false blow may shatter a precious fossil into particles too small to be recovered.

Before any bones are removed, the fossil hunters number and photograph them, and chart their positions in the rock. When the individual bones have been taken out, these records will help laboratory workers to fit them back together in the proper order.

Once a fossil bone has been bared, the fossil hunters paint it with a thin preserving coat of shellac. Then they stick on layers of thin rice paper or tissue paper. Next, they swathe the bone in sacking coated with plaster of Paris. Lastly, they plaster thick stick splints on the outside of the package. Removing an entire fossil dinosaur usually means cutting free its bones in many separate blocks and treating each one individually. Splinted and bandaged like broken human legs or arms, the fossils are at last protected for their journey back to a museum.

In the Museum

Finding and freeing a fossil dinosaur may take several seasons of work. This simply launches a long process of study. Years of laboratory work may follow before the bones of a skeleton can be fully cleaned, linked together and scientifically understood. Only then may the true size, shape and nature of a hitherto unknown beast become clear.

Often the fossils arrive at the laboratory still embedded in stone. Getting rid of this stone is the job of skilled technicians. First, they

Between 1963 and 1971, a series of joint Polish-Mongolian expeditions explored the rich fossil beds of Mongolia. They excavated some magnificent dinosaurs and even some mammal fossils of the late Cretaceous Period. Here the eggs of a Protoceratops are being excavated.

Opposite page: A worker at Dinosaur National Monument in Utah uses hammer and chisel to bring a Camarasaurus shoulder blade into sharp relief against the rock surface. Visitors to the Monument can see a variety of dinosaur bones still embedded in the rock in which they were found.

These pictures were taken in 1963 during a British expedition to Central Africa. Above left: A scientist cleans loose rock from around the skull of a fossil dinosaur.

Above right: The fossil is coated with layers of wet tissue paper, after which layers of sacking soaked in plaster of Paris are laid down over the specimen (left). The tissue paper prevents the plaster from adhering to the fossil.

Below left: Each specimen must be carefully marked so that scientists know exactly where it was found. It must then be put in a separate bag before being packed in a strong wooden box which protects the fossils on their long journey to the nearest seaport (below right).

soak off the protective sacking and paper bandages. Then they set to work to chip away the unwanted stone. Their tool kit is varied and impressive. They may tap away with hammer and chisel, but mechanical aids help them to work faster. One of these is the so-called air hammer. Another tool, rather like a high-speed dentist's drill, vibrates 30,000 times per second, faster than the speed of sound. A third process is based on sand blasting, in which a jet of compressed air containing sand blasts impurities from metal surfaces. Skilfully applied, an abrasive jet can cut the finest fossil bones from the stone in which they lie embedded.

Mounting Exhibits

Sometimes careful excavation and laboratory work combine to salvage a dinosaur skeleton intact, and the museum may decide to mount the skeleton in a lifelike pose. By studying the shapes and sizes of its bones anatomists can work out how the

creature would have stood. The next step is to prop up the huge, heavy bones in this position. Some sort of scaffolding is necessary to hold them all together. Craftsmen heat and bend steel or iron rods and fashion metal clamps. Their object is to make supports shaped so that people can see as much of the skeleton and as little of its supporting ironmongery as possible. Several men may work full time for months to erect a big dinosaur skeleton.

Reconstructing the Past

For most of us these proofs that there were monsters in the prehistoric past provide an enjoyable day's outing. But to the palaeontologists who work behind the scenes, fossils are a life's study. Each type of fossil may conceal a mine of information.

Take bones, for instance. The numbers and positions of bones found in rocks gives some idea of where and when each dinosaur lived, and whether it was plentiful. Grooves, scars and bumps on bones show where, long ago, the muscles were attached. It is the careful study of these tell-tale marks that helps experts to work out the shapes and sizes of the animals. They can then make scale models from which they are able to work out the creatures' volumes and weights. These sums have cut the original guessed-at weight of *Diplodocus* by 20 tonnes, but have made *Brachiosaurus* 30 tonnes heavier than was thought.

Bone studies also help palaeontologists to work out how the dinosaurs lived. From holes in skulls they can tell the sizes of the eyes, ears, nasal passages, and brain. These give a good idea of how well a dinosaur could see, hear, smell and think. Examination of skulls has also shown that dinosaurs, unlike reptiles, could breathe while they ate, as mammals do.

But some of the most exciting information has come from studies of the limb bones. By the 1960s the creatures' long leg bones and upright stance set some scientists wondering what kind of animals the dinosaurs really were. The longer and more upright the leg bones of animals, the likelier are creatures to run fast and far. Were dinosaurs as energetic as their leg bones suggested? People had always called them reptiles. But reptiles can only run in short bursts. They lack the rich blood supply needed for long spells of active movement.

Warm or Cold Blooded?

More bone studies brought a possible answer. Slices cut from dinosaur bone revealed channels where blood had flowed. Scientists found that dinosaurs had had a much more abundant blood supply than any lizard, crocodile or turtle.

By the 1970s finds like these had convinced at least some palaeontologists that all dinosaurs had been active, warm-blooded animals. These scientists have therefore argued that dinosaurs should no longer be lumped with the cold-blooded, relatively sluggish reptiles. The dinosaurs, they say, rank

Below: Fossil dinosaur footprint (left) and bone, in this case the skull of a bonehead, still embedded in rock. The study of such evidence helps experts to judge the shape, size and attitude of long-vanished beasts. They may even be able to tell how these creatures walked or ran.

Discovering what dinosaurs
really looked like is by no
means always easy. As they
occur in rock (above) the
jumbled bones and bony
plates of a Stegosaurus may
give us only some of the
clues to how it stood or how
the plates fitted on its back.

Above: Careful study of the
jumbled bones fossilized in rock
enable an anatomist to discover
how most of them fitted together.
Intelligent guesswork helps him to
work out how the rest were
arranged. His studies eventually
make it possible to reconstruct the
entire skeleton.

Left: By noting tell-tale
marks where muscles
joined bones, experts can
remodel Stegosaurus's
whole body.

Right: Anyone who knows
an elephant only from its
skeleton would never guess
that the creature had its
nostrils at the tip of a long,
flexible trunk that also
served as a muscular fifth
limb. Similarly, a dinosaur's
skeleton does not tell us
everything about its owner.
Some dinosaurs may have
had trunks, too.

as a major group of animals on their own.

But other scientists studying the same bone material came up with different findings. For instance, they argue that bone structure shows how fast the creature grew, not how fast the creature burned up energy when adult. Similarly, they argue, upright posture need not imply the energy for running. Scientists who stress these findings suggest that the dinosaurs could not have been warm blooded, like living mammals. But many of them think that dinosaurs were not like any reptiles now alive.

Bone damage is another source of knowledge about dinosaurs. The study known as palaeopathology shows, for instance, that some sauropods had broken ribs that later mended. One *Iguanodon* had a similar repair to its hip girdle. Horned dinosaurs suffered injuries to their massive, armoured heads. One *Allosaurus* specimen had a damaged shoulder blade covered by an overgrowth of bone. One hadrosaur had a wound that got infected, producing an enormous abscess on its foreleg. Bacteria attacked the tail bones in an *Apatosaurus*. Big sauropods were also sometimes victims of arthritis.

Very rarely, the soft parts of the body survive as fossils. A skin imprint on brownish sandstone revealed the plates and spikes guarding *Scolosaurus*'s back. A similar impression showed up the duckbill *Anatosaurus*'s leathery, pebbly-patterned skin.

Fossil footprints, too, have tales to tell. Some match the feet of known types of dinosaurs. The tracks help us to judge how these beasts stood, walked, ran, swam and rested. From the kind of rock that bears their tracks we can sometimes tell if the dinosaurs were walking on a wet mudflat, or on mud baked hard by sunshine. But what is most tantalizing is that the makers of most fossil footprints remain unknown.

Also, we can only guess at which dinosaurs laid some of the fossil eggs that scientists have found. We do know, though, that in late Cretaceous times, some dinosaur eggshells held too little calcium to supply skeletons for the embryos inside them. Thus the babies never hatched. What made the mothers lay imperfect eggs? And were infertile eggs a reason why dinosaurs became extinct?

Dinosaurs died out some 65 million years ago but the mysteries they left behind still fascinate us. Solving these mysteries offers one of the most exciting challenges that fossil hunters face today.

The fossil record of an African dinosaur's meanderings where Lesotho lies today. There are still many dinosaur mysteries to probe. We can never know for certain which genus of dinosaur made each type of footprint.

Glossary

A

ACANTHOPHOLIS An armoured dinosaur that lived in early Cretaceous times. Flattish bony plates covered its back and tail. Small spines may have bristled from the shoulders.

AGE OF REPTILES Another name for the Mesozoic Era, when reptiles dominated the world's land and seas.

ALLOSAURUS This carnosaur, whose name means 'leaping reptile', lived in the late Jurassic Period. It is also known as *Antrodemus*. It had blade-like fangs and each forelimb bore three large 'fingers' armed with long claws.

AMINO ACID An organic compound characterized by the presence in its molecules of both the acidic carboxyl group (COOH) and the basic or 'amino' group NH_2. Amino acids play a vital part in the chemistry of life. They are the building bricks of proteins.

AMMONITES Relatives of octopus and squid, with a flat, spiral shell, that evolved in the Palaeozoic Era and flourished during Mesozoic times. Ammonites became extinct at the end of the Cretaceous Period.

AMPHIBIAN Moist-skinned animal that lives in both water and air. Frogs, newts and salamanders breed and lay eggs in water. They have gills during the early part of their lives, and can breathe under water, but the adult animals can leave the water to breathe air.

ANKYLOSAURS A group of armoured dinosaurs with low, squat, heavy bodies, the name meaning 'rounded reptiles' from the curved shapes of their ribs. They survived until the end of the Cretaceous Period.

ANNING, MARY (1799–1847) One of the earliest professional fossil hunters. At the age of 11 she found the first almost complete fossil of an ichthyosaur embedded in sea cliffs at Lyme Regis in southern England, where she lived. She went on to discover plesiosaur and pterodactyl fossils.

ANTRODEMUS See **ALLOSAURUS**.

APATOSAURUS A giant sauropod dinosaur once known as *Brontosaurus* ('thunder lizard'). It was about 25 metres (80 feet) long and weighed over 30 tonnes, five times as much as a modern elephant.

ARCHAEOPTERYX The first recorded bird. It was crow sized, with a long reptilian tail, narrow beak-shaped jaws with teeth, and clawed fingers projecting forwards from its wings. Jurassic Period.

ARCHELON The largest turtle that ever lived, 4 metres (13 feet) long, of the late Cretaceous Period. Its protective, yet lightweight, shell gave it mobility and defence.

B

ARCHOSAURS All dinosaurs came from a group of reptiles called archosaurs. Today's crocodiles are the only living archosaurs, but the early archosaurs' descendants, the birds, are some of the most successful of all animals.

ARTHROPOD An invertebrate animal with a jointed body and limbs. Insects, spiders and lobsters are all arthropods, as were the now extinct trilobites.

BLUE-GREEN ALGAE Any of a class of the simple plants called algae that have their chlorophyll masked by bluish-green pigments.

BONE-HEADED DINOSAUR A bird-hipped, bipedal herbivore which lived in Cretaceous North America, Asia and Europe. Its thick skull was used as a duelling weapon.

BRACHIOPODS Marine invertebrates with a bivalve shell. They have a pair of tentacles inside the shell which they use to bring microscopic food to the mouth. Brachiopods are commonly called lamp shells because the larger of their two shells has an opening like the wick-hole in a Roman oil lamp.

BRACHIOSAURUS A large sauropod, the heaviest dinosaur of them all. Some individuals may have weighed 100 tonnes, equal to about 20 large elephants. *Brachiosaurus* must have spent most of its time eating to sustain its enormous bulk. Unlike most other dinosaurs, its front legs were longer than its hind legs. Jurassic Period.

BRONTOSAURUS See **APATOSAURUS**.

C

CAMARASAURUS A sauropod whose name means 'chambered lizard' from the hollow chambers in its backbone. *Camarasaurus'* front legs were longer than its hind legs. A fossil of a young *Camarasaurus* was found in Utah in 1922. Jurassic Period.

CAMBRIAN PERIOD A period of geological time; the first period of the Palaeozoic Era. During the Cambrian Period a wide variety of complex living things evolved, but no backboned creatures. Trilobites dominated the seas.

CAMPTOSAURUS A large, bird-hipped, herbivorous dinosaur. It could stand on its hind limbs balanced by its heavy tail, with its shortish forelimbs held up off the ground. When moving slowly it probably went down on all fours. Jurassic to Cretaceous.

CARBONIFEROUS PERIOD The fifth period of the Palaeozoic Era. It is so named from the vast seams of coal

(carbon) produced from the remains of plants that lived during this time. The period saw the spread of amphibians and the rise of the reptiles. Insects appeared and became common.

CARNIVORE A flesh-eating animal.

CARNOSAURS A group of lizard-hipped, flesh-eating dinosaurs descended from *Ornithosuchus*. They were powerful animals with massive heads armed with dagger-like teeth. The biggest carnosaur was *Tyrannosaurus*.

CENOZOIC ERA A major division of geological time — the Age of Recent Life. It extends from the end of the Mesozoic Era to the present.

CERATOPSIANS Horned dinosaurs, similar to rhinoceroses, that were the last group of dinosaurs to develop.

CETIOSAURUS The first fossil sauropod dinosaur to be found — near Oxford, England, in the 1830s. It was as heavy as three elephants and measured 18 metres (60 feet) from head to tail. Jurassic to Cretaceous.

CHASMOSAURUS A long-frilled ceratopsian dinosaur with a small nasal horn and two big horns that jutted from its brow. It appeared during the late Cretaceous Period.

CLUBMOSS A plant related to the fern, so called from the club-like form of the spike where spores are carried. Clubmosses first appeared in the Devonian Period and grew to enormous proportions in the Carboniferous Period -- some of them were 30 metres (100 feet) tall, with trunks up to 2 metres (6 feet) in diameter.

COELOPHYSIS One of the earliest known dinosaurs, it was a slender creature about 2 to 3 metres (8 feet) in length. It ran on its hind legs and used its forelimbs for grasping its prey. Triassic Period.

COELUROSAURS A group of carnivorous dinosaurs descended from *Coelophysis*. Unlike the carnosaurs, they relied on long legs for speed and agility to catch their prey. Their long-fingered 'hands' were designed to grasp small animals.

COELURUS A Jurassic coelurosaur, also called *Ornitholestes*. Somewhat longer than a man, it weighed much less. It had a small, low skull and a long neck balanced by an even longer tail. *Coelurus* ran on its hind legs with neck outstretched.

COMPSOGNATHUS Small Jurassic coelurosaurs, some scarcely bigger than a hen. They resembled a slender, agile, wingless bird. Their forelimbs normally bore three-clawed fingers, though one type apparently evolved flippers instead of 'hands'.

CONIFERS Any of an order of mostly evergreen trees and shrubs, including pines. They carry seeds in woody cones.

CONTINENTAL DRIFT The term used to

describe the continuous slow movement of the earth's continents, caused by the shifting of the separate 'plates' of the earth's crust on which they lie. During the Mesozoic Era what had been a single supercontinent gradually broke up, and the continents drifted to their modern positions.

COPE, EDWARD (1840–1897) American palaeontologist, bitter rival of Othniel Marsh. Cope led a team which prised hundreds of sauropod fossil bones from Jurassic rock in the western USA.

COTYLOSAURS A group of early reptiles of the late Palaeozoic Era and the Triassic Period. They are often called the *stem reptiles* because they gave rise to all other reptiles.

CRETACEOUS PERIOD The third and last period of the Mesozoic Era. During this time the dinosaurs continued to dominate the land, and then became extinct. There were many small mammals and birds.

CYCAD A member of a class of gymnosperm plants, with thick, unbranched trunks and long, fern-like leaves. Cycads were widespread in Mesozoic times, when many of them were large and tree-like. Today's cycads are only a few feet high.

D

DEVONIAN PERIOD The fourth period of the Palaeozoic Era. The age of fishes — many kinds abundant in fresh and salt water. Amphibians evolved from fishes and moved on to the land.

DICYNODONTS The first plant-eating, mammal-like reptiles. They had a single pair of tusk-like teeth in their upper jaw. Dicynodonts developed early in the Permian Period.

DIMETRODON A carnivorous pelycosaur reptile that lived in Permian times. It had a large 'sail' on its back, supported by spikes growing from its backbone. Between the spikes stretched a web of skin. It is thought that this sail acted like a radiator, helping the animal to control its temperature.

DINOSAUR A term meaning 'terrible lizard', used to refer to any of a group of extinct carnivorous or herbivorous reptiles that dominated life on earth from 225 million to about 65 million years ago. Dinosaurs are divided into two main groups: 'lizard-hipped' (saurischians) and 'bird-hipped' (ornithischians), according to their pelvic structure.

DIPLODOCUS This big Jurassic plant-eating sauropod was the longest land animal ever to have lived. It grew up to 27 metres (88 feet) in length, with a 14-metre (45-foot) whip-like tail.

DSUNGARIPTERUS An early Cretaceous winged reptile. It had a 3-metre (10-foot) wingspan and its spiky-tipped jaws were probably designed for spearing fish.

DUCK-BILLED DINOSAURS See **HADROSAURS**.

E–F

ELASMOSAURUS A long-necked plesiosaur that swam in late Cretaceous seas. It had 76 vertebrae in its flexible neck, which was more than half the total length of its body. *Elasmosaurus* grew to more than 12 metres (40 feet) in overall length.

EPOCH In geological time, a subdivision of a period.

ERA A major division of geological time. The Precambrian Era lasted from the earth's birth to the beginning of the Palaeozoic Era — about 4000 million years. The Palaeozoic Era was followed by the Mesozoic and Cenozoic Eras. The eras are divided into periods.

EUOPLOCEPHALUS A low, heavy, armoured dinosaur that lived in late Cretaceous times. It may have looked something like a gigantic tortoise.

EUPARKERIA One of the earliest archosaurs, this Triassic reptile was able to run on its hind legs and used its tail to counterbalance the weight of its body.

FABROSAURUS This first known ornithischian dinosaur was a metre (3 feet) in length, with long back legs and short front ones. It lived during the Triassic Period.

FLOWERING PLANTS Plants that produce flowers, fruits and seeds; also called angiosperms.

FOSSIL The remains of an animal or plant that have been preserved in the earth's crust, often in petrified form.

G

GEOSAURUS An early crocodile of the Jurassic seas. It had seal-like flippers and a tail fin like an ichthyosaur's.

GINKGO A gymnosperm with fan-shaped leaves, also known as a maidenhair tree. The Mesozoic ancestors of the modern ginkgo flourished over wide areas in Jurassic times.

GONDWANALAND The major land mass that made up the southern part of the supercontinent Pangaea in Triassic times. It included present-day Africa, South America, India, Australia and Antarctica.

H

HADROSAURS Bipedal dinosaurs of the Cretaceous Period which lived in all northern continents. They averaged around 9 metres (30 feet) long, and walked on strong hind legs. Known as 'duck-billed' dinosaurs from their wide, toothless beaks, the hadrosaurs found their food on land. They are grouped according to their varying head crests.

HERBIVORE A plant-eating animal.

HORSETAIL A flowerless and leafless plant related to ferns. In Carboniferous times ancestors of the horsetails formed dense forests 30 metres (100 feet) high.

HYLONOMUS An early reptile which appeared in the Carboniferous Period. It looked like a clumsy lizard, and lived most of its life in the water, but laid its shelled eggs on land.

HYPSILOPHODON A bird-hipped bipedal dinosaur 2 metres (6 feet) long. It had a row of small teeth at the front end of the upper jaw and cheek teeth for grinding vegetation. It probably ran faster than any other dinosaur and survived because it was able to outrun its enemies.

I–J

ICHTHYOSAURS A group of marine reptiles that appeared in the late Triassic Period and survived until the late Cretaceous Period. They reached a length of 10 metres (33 feet) and were powerful swimmers. They resembled modern dolphins in appearance.

IGUANODON A herbivorous biped, 8 metres (26 feet) long, of early Cretaceous times. It had crowded rows of teeth for pulping leaves. Its forelimbs were small but its long thumbs evolved as spikes.

INVERTEBRATE An animal lacking a spinal column. All Protozoa are invertebrates, as are such creatures as sponges, jellyfish, flatworms, shellfish, octopuses, earthworms, insects, spiders and crabs.

JELLYFISH A free-swimming coelenterate with an almost transparent saucer-shaped body and tentacles studded with stinging cells. Forerunners of the jellyfish lived in Precambrian times.

JURASSIC PERIOD The second of the three periods of the Mesozoic Era. During this period the dinosaurs were abundant on land; the first birds appeared.

K–L

KRONOSAURUS A 17-metre (56-foot) long sea reptile of Cretaceous times that fed on other marine reptiles.

KUEHNEOSAURUS A Triassic lizard that took to the air. It had skin flaps which allowed it to glide for short distances.

LABYRINTHODONT An early type of amphibian. Some were tiny, others grew as large as crocodiles. From these large labyrinthodonts evolved the reptiles.

LAURASIA The major land mass that made up the northern part of the supercontinent Pangaea in Triassic times. It included present-day Europe, Asia and North America.

LEPOSPONDYLS A group of primitive amphibians which lived in Carboniferous times. Some spent all their lives in water, others had stout limbs and spent most of their time on dry land. From the latter group came the ancestors of modern amphibians.

LOBE-FINNED FISH The lobe-fins take their name from the fact that their fins are carried on short, scale-covered legs. They were the first land-living vertebrates. The rhipidistians, coelacanths and lungfishes are all lobe-finned fishes.

LYCAENOPS A carnivorous mammal-like reptile of the late Permian Period. It had long legs which allowed it to chase and catch the clumsier plant-eaters.

LYSTROSAURUS A plant-eating mammal-like reptile of the early Triassic. It lived a semi-aquatic existence, rather as a hippopotamus does today.

M

MAMMAL Any of a class of higher vertebrates, including man. Mammals feed their young with milk secreted by mammary glands and their skin is usually more or less covered by hair.

MAMMAL-LIKE REPTILES Reptiles smaller than most dinosaurs that dominated the land at the beginning of the Permian Period. They eventually gave rise to the mammals.

MANTELL, GIDEON (1790–1852) A British country doctor with a passion for collecting fossils. In 1822 he discovered some large fossilized teeth among rocks he knew to be Cretaceous. Realizing that the teeth looked very like those of the living iguana lizard, but much larger, he called the fossil *Iguanodon* ('iguana tooth'). *Iguanodon* was the first dinosaur to be identified and described as such.

MEGALOSAURS A family of medium to large flesh-eaters which appeared early in the Jurassic Period.

MESOZOIC ERA A major division of geological time – the Age of Middle Life. It is made up of the Triassic, Jurassic and Cretaceous periods and was followed by the Cenozoic Era. The dinosaurs evolved and vanished in the Mesozoic Era, which is also called the Age of Reptiles.

MICROSAUR A kind of lepospondyl, an amphibian of the late Carboniferous Period. It had legs and may have given rise to today's salamanders, frogs and toads.

MOLLUSC A soft-bodied invertebrate, usually with a hard protective shell. The molluscs include snails, mussels, cuttlefish, slugs and the octopus.

MONOCLONIUS A short-frilled ceratopsian with a long, strong, nasal horn and a pair of tiny bumps on the forehead. Late Cretaceous Period.

MOSASAURS Giant sea-going lizards, 15 metres (48 feet) long, of the late Cretaceous Period. They fed chiefly on cephalopods.

MOULD A type of fossil formed when water dissolves the body of a creature, leaving a hollow in the rock in which it is embedded. The hollow preserves the shape of the vanished animal.

N–O

NOTHOSAURS A group of marine reptiles that flourished in Triassic times. They ranged from 40 cm (1½ feet) to 6 metres (20 feet) in length, and had a back fin and webbed feet.

NUCLEIC ACID Any of various acids such as DNA or RNA found in the nuclei of living cells.

ORDOVICIAN PERIOD The second period of the Palaeozoic Era. It was named after a Welsh tribe in whose area rocks of the period were first recognized.

ORNITHISCHIANS A term, meaning 'bird-hipped', used to refer to one of the two main groups of dinosaurs, distinguished by the structure of their pelvic girdles.

ORNITHOLESTES See **COELURUS**.

ORNITHOMIMUS One of a closely related group of big coelurosaurian dinosaurs of ostrich-like appearance that stood more than 2 metres (6 feet) high. Probably omnivorous, it moved on two long hind legs and had arms ending in clawed 'hands'.

ORNITHOPODS Herbivorous, bird-hipped dinosaurs which reached their climax in Cretaceous times. One line consisted of four-legged beasts and the other group largely went around on hind legs only.

ORNITHOSUCHUS Triassic ancestor of the carnosaurs. Some experts believe it was the first flesh-eating dinosaur. It was up to 3 metres (10 feet) long and it walked on only two legs, balancing its body with its tail.

OWEN, RICHARD (1804–1892) A British anatomist and zoologist, Owen carried out a comprehensive study of huge reptilian bones. He was first to use the word *dinosaur*, meaning 'terrible lizard'.

P

PACHYCEPHALOSAURUS The largest of the bone-headed, plant-eating dinosaurs. Sharp knobs projected from the skull back, and short, bony spikes stuck up from its beak-like snout. Cretaceous Period.

PACHYRHINOSAURUS A hornless ceratopsian dinosaur with thick bone shielding the upper front part of its head. It lived during the late Cretaceous Period.

PALAEONTOLOGY The study of the life of past geological times as known from fossil remains.

PALAEOSCINCUS The most heavily armoured ankylosaur, it had flat, bony plates encased in its back and a row of spikes jutting outwards from its sides. Cretaceous Period.

PALAEOZOIC ERA A major division of geological time – the Age of Ancient Life. It extended from the Cambrian through the Permian periods and was followed by the Mesozoic Era.

PANGAEA The giant supercontinent which, before the Mesozoic Era began, contained all the land masses of the earth.

PELYCOSAURS An offshoot group from the cotylosaur stem, these reptiles, which included *Dimetrodon*, had a skin 'sail' on their backs which acted as a heat radiator. Permian Period.

PENTACERATOPS A long-frilled ceratopsian dinosaur of the late Cretaceous Period with large horns and an extra pair of horn-like bony knobs projecting from the cheeks.

PERIOD In geological time, a subdivision of an era. The dinosaurs evolved in the Triassic Period and died out in the Cretaceous Period – all in the Mesozoic Era.

PERMIAN PERIOD The geological period that ended the Palaeozoic Era. During this period the reptiles increased and spread. Trilobites became extinct.

PHOBOSUCHUS At about 15 metres (50 feet), the biggest crocodilian ever to have lived. It preyed upon dinosaurs in late Cretaceous North America.

PHOTOSYNTHESIS A process by which plants combine water, carbon dioxide and minerals to make food. It depends on the presence of a complex green pigment called chlorophyll and relies on the energy of sunlight.

PHYTOSAURS A group of flesh-eating archosaurs of the Triassic Period. They looked and lived much like the modern crocodile.

PLACODONTS A group of Triassic marine reptiles. They probably lived in shallow water around coasts. Their squat bodies were protected by heavy armour and they used their strong front teeth to gather and crush molluscs.

PLATEOSAURUS A large plant-eating dinosaur that lived in the late Triassic Period. It was 6 metres (20 feet) in length. *Plateosaurus* reared up to browse on leaves growing high off the ground, and some scientists believe that it was the first warm-blooded dinosaur. It may have given rise to the sauropods.

PLESIOSAURS A group of marine reptiles. They reached a length of over 12 metres (40 feet) and propelled themselves through the water with powerful strokes of their paddle-shaped limbs. Plesiosaurs are divided into two groups – long-necked and short-necked (pliosaurs). They lived in the Mesozoic Era.

PLIOSAURS Voracious, short-necked plesiosaurs that lived in Cretaceous seas and fed on other marine creatures, including long-necked plesiosaurs. *Kronosaurus* was a pliosaur.

POLACANTHUS An armour-plated dinosaur, resembling a gigantic armadillo, which lived in early Cretaceous times. It had a heavy tail, powerful limbs and a small head.

PRECAMBRIAN ERA A major era of geological time. It extends from the birth of the earth to the Cambrian Period that began the Palaeozoic Era — some 4000 million years.

PROGANOCHELYS A marine turtle of the late Triassic Period that wore a heavy, bony 'overcoat', sacrificing mobility for safety.

PROTEIN Any of a large number of highly complex organic compounds. They are essential to life, forming most of the tissues of living organisms, and they regulate the working of the body. Proteins are also an essential part of the food eaten by higher organisms.

PROTEROSUCHUS One of the first archosaurs and an ancestor of the dinosaurs. It lived in rivers and lakes and behaved much like the modern crocodile.

PROTOCERATOPS The first true frilled dinosaur, ancestor of the later ceratopsians. About 2 metres (6 feet) long, it lived during the late Cretaceous Period. Its collar formed a big shield over its neck and shoulders.

PSITTACOSAURUS A two-legged, plant-eating dinosaur, forerunner of the true horned dinosaurs, or ceratopsians. Longer than a man, it had a deep skull, ending in a 'parrot beak' that gave it its name. Cretaceous Period.

PTERANODON A Cretaceous gliding winged reptile with a wingspread of over 7 metres (24 feet). Its body was no longer than a turkey's.

PTERODACTYLUS A small flying reptile of the late Jurassic Period. It had a short tail, a horny beak and long wing bones.

PTEROSAURS A group of Mesozoic winged reptiles. Some were sparrow-sized; others would have dwarfed the largest eagle.

Q–R

QUETZALCOATLUS A giant winged reptile discovered in Texas in 1975. Its wingspan may have been as much as 15 metres (50 feet) and it probably soared and fed as modern vultures do.

REPTILE Any of a class of air-breathing vertebrates that include the alligators and crocodiles, lizards, snakes and turtles. The body is usually covered with scales or bony plates.

RHAMPHORHYNCHOIDS A group of winged reptiles from the Jurassic Period. With fairly short, broad wings, they resembled crows, though some had very long tails.

RHIPIDISTIANS A group of flesh-eating, lobe-finned fishes which gave rise to the amphibians. The rhipidistians were common in Devonian times and

reached a length of 3 metres (10 feet) or more. They had lungs and could breathe air.

RHYNCHOSAUR A reptile that evolved during the Triassic Period. It had a beak-like mouth with large teeth and its fossil remains have been found in most parts of the world.

S

SAURISCHIANS A general name for all dinosaurs, both flesh-eating and plant-eating, which were 'lizard-hipped', as opposed to the 'bird-hipped' ornithischians.

SAUROPODS A group of plant-eating dinosaurs. They were the longest and heaviest reptiles that ever lived. Their huge bodies tapered to a long neck at one end and a long tail at the other. *Brachiosaurus*, *Apatosaurus* (*Brontosaurus*) and *Diplodocus* were members of the sauropod group.

SCELIDOSAURUS A four-legged, bony-plated herbivore, ancestor of the armoured dinosaurs — the stegosaurs and ankylosaurs. Low, bony plates arranged like stepping stones studded its back from head to tail. Jurassic Period.

SCOLOSAURUS A large ankylosaur that lived in the Cretaceous Period. With its massive bony spikes it was well protected, the biggest spikes being the two that jutted from the end of its tail. It resembled a gigantic spiky tortoise.

SEDIMENTARY ROCKS Rocks formed from sediments of fine mud and sand deposited in seas and lakes. The sediment becomes compressed as new layers are deposited over the old. Millions of years of the earth's history are locked in the layers of sedimentary rock.

SILURIAN PERIOD The third period of the Palaeozoic Era. During this period the first jawed fishes appeared; also the first land plants.

SORDES PILOSUS A winged reptile from the Jurassic Period whose name means 'hairy devil'. A body covering of fur acted as an insulating layer and provided more energy for flight.

SPINOSAURUS A 12-metre (39-foot) long carnosaur that lived in Cretaceous times. It had spines longer than a man's body on its back, with a web of skin stretched between them.

STEGOCERAS A bone-headed dinosaur no taller than a man. From the back of its skull jutted a low bony frill. Cretaceous Period.

STEGOSAURS Armoured plant-eating dinosaurs with enormous bony plates and spikes on their bodies that lived during the Jurassic Period.

STEGOSAURUS The largest of the stegosaurs, this dinosaur roamed Jurassic North America and fed on the lush vegetation that abounded there. Two rows of triangular bony plates jutted from its back, and two pairs of bony

spikes encased in horn projected sideways from its tail.

STYRACOSAURUS Known as 'spiny reptile', this ceratopsian of the late Cretaceous Period had a long nasal horn and an elaborate frill edged with spikes.

T

TANYSTROPHEUS A reptile that lived in and by the sea during the Triassic Period. It had a long, tubular neck and fed on fish and molluscs by plunging its small head under water.

TELEOSAURUS A crocodilian of the Jurassic seas, with long, slim, sharp-toothed jaws for seizing fish.

THECODONTOSAURUS Possibly the first dinosaur to eat plants as well as animals. Its fossil skeleton, 2–3 metres (7 feet) long, has been found in Triassic rocks in parts of Germany and England.

THEROPODS A group of flesh-eating dinosaurs comprising the coelurosaurs and the carnosaurs.

TICINOSUCHUS A long, low, carnivorous reptile of Triassic times. It walked and ran on all four legs. Many scientists believe that *Ticinosuchus* was the ancestor of the sauropods.

TOROSAURUS The largest of the long-frilled dinosaurs, with enormous brow horns and a frill that reached beyond its shoulders. It lived during the late Cretaceous Period.

TRIASSIC PERIOD The first period of the Mesozoic Era. During this time the reptiles evolved to produce the first dinosaurs and large marine reptiles. The first mammals evolved.

TRICERATOPS The last and largest of all ceratopsian dinosaurs. It was over 7 metres (24 feet) long and resembled a huge rhinoceros. Its nasal horn was short, but a pair of horns almost a metre (3 feet) long projected from its brows.

TRILOBITE An early Palaeozoic marine arthropod. The segments of its body were divided by furrows into three lobes. Trilobites dominated Cambrian seas.

TYRANNOSAURUS The largest carnivorous dinosaur. It was about 15 metres (50 feet) long and stood about 6 metres (20 feet) high on its strong back legs. *Tyrannosaurus'* huge mouth held dagger-like teeth; its heavy tail may have been used to help it balance. Cretaceous Period.

V

VELOCIRAPTOR A long-legged, predatory dinosaur with grasping hands, belonging to the coelurosaur group. Cretaceous Period.

VERTEBRATE An animal with a skull and backbone. About 43,000 species of vertebrate are known, including bony fishes, amphibians, reptiles, birds and mammals.

Index

Figures in *italic* refer to illustrations.

A
Acanthopholis 63
Alamosaurus 79
Allosaurus 26, 42, 44
Altan Ula *85*
ammonite 80
amphibians *18*, 20, 21, *22*, 22–23
Anatosaurus 13, *57*
animals, first appearance of 17
ankylosaurs 63, 64
Ankylosaurus see *Euoplocephalus*
Anning, Mary 9
Antrodemus see *Allosaurus*
Apatosaurus 32, 35
Archaeopteryx 26, *46*, 49
Archelon 27, 77, *77*
archosaurs 28, *28*, 29, *29*, 31
'arm lizard' see *Brachiosaurus*
armoured dinosaurs 61, *67*, 80
Arthropleura 21
arthropod 19, 21

B
Barosaurus 35, *37*
Bighorn ram *54*
'bird-hipped' dinosaurs see ornithischians
birds 7, *26*, 27, *27*, 28, *31*, *46*, 47, 82
bone 87, *88*
bone-headed dinosaur 54, *54–55*, 80, *87*
Brachiosaurus 32, 33, 38
Brontosaurus see *Apatosaurus*

C
Camarasaurus 33, *35*, 38, *84*
Cambrian Period *14*, 16, *16*, 17
Camptosaurus 50, 51, *51*
captorhinomorphs 23
Carboniferous Period *14*, 20, *20*
carnosaurs 23, 29, 30, *40*, 41, 44, *49*
cell 17
Cenozoic Era 14, *14–15*
Cephalaspis 17
cephalopods *17*
ceratopsians 64, 66
Cetiosaurus 32, 33, *33*, 40
'chambered lizard' see *Camarasaurus*
Chasmosaurus 66
clubmoss *20*
coal forest 20, *20*

Coelophysis 28, 29
coelurosaurs *28*, 29, 30, 45, *46*, 49, *49*
Coelurus (Ornitholestes) 45, 46
Como Bluff, Wyoming *11*
Compsognathus 37, 46, *46*
continents, movement of 26, 27, 82
Cope, Edward Drinker *12*, 13
Corythosaurus 50, 57
cotylosaurs 23
Cretaceous Period *14–15*, 27, *27*, 42, *45*, 49, 51, 53, 54, 57, 63, 64, *67*, 71, 77, 79, 81, *81*, 82, *83*
crocodilians 28, *28*, 31, *76*, 77
crustacean *16*
Crystal Palace *10*, 12
cycad *26*

D
Deinodon horridus 13
Deinonychus 45
Devonian Period *14*, 18, *18–19*
diadectomorphs 23
dicynodonts 23, *23*
Dimetrodon 22
Dimorphodon 69
Dinosaur National Monument, Utah *84*
Dinosaurs, Age of 25, 72, 77
Diplodocus 12, *26*, *34*, 35
Dsungaripterus 71
duck-billed dinosaurs see hadrosaurs

E
earth, ages of the 14, *14–15*
echinoderm *16*
Edmontosaurus 58
egg *23*, *39*, *65*, 66, *79*, 89
Elasmosaurus 27, 76
elephant *37*, *88*
Eogyrinus 21
epoch 14
era 14
Euoplocephalus 62, 63
Euparkeria 28, *28*

F
Fabrosaurus 30, *30*
ferns 21
fin *18*
fish *17*, 18
'fish lizard' see *Ichthyosaurus*
Flood, Biblical 9
flowering plants 27
footprints 12, *35*, 36, *41*, *87*, 89, *89*

forest 20, *20*, 33
fossil 7, *8*, 9, 11, 12, *13*, *16*, *17*, *39*, *41*, *46*, *63*, *75*, *82*, *84*, 85, *85*, *86*, *87*, *88*

G – H
Geosaurus 77
Gondwanaland 25
Gorgosaurus 44, *62*
hadrosaurs *9*, 42, 57, *57*, 58, *59*, *76*, 82
Hawkins, Waterhouse *10*, 11
Hay, Oliver P. 34
Hayden, Ferdinand 13
herbivores 23, 29, 44, 51
Hesperornis 27, 71
hip girdle 30, *30*
hippopotamus 37
Holland, W. J. 34
horned dinosaurs 64, *67*, 79, 82
horsetail *20*
Hylaeosaurus 10
Hylonomus 21, 23
Hypsilophodon 52, 54
hypsilophodonts *59*

I – J
Ichthyornis 71
ichthyosaurs 9, 74, 76, 80, 82
Ichthyosaurus 26, 74, *74*, *75*
Ichthyostega 19
Iguanodon 10, 11, *50*, 53, *53*
iguanodonts *59*
invertebrates 17, *80*
jellyfish *16*
Jurassic Period *14–15*, 26, *26*, 33, 36, 42, 45, *46*, *50*, 61, *67*, 69, *69*, 71, 77

K – L
Kentrosaurus 62
Kritosaurs 58
Kronosaurus 76
Kuehneosaurus 26
labyrinthodonts 21, *21*, 22
Lakes, Arthur *11*, 13
Lambe, L. M. 58
Lambeosaurines 58, *58*
Lambeosaurus 58, *58*, *59*
'leaping reptile' see *Allosaurus*
Leidy, Joseph 13
lepospondyls 21, *21*
Leptoceratops 64
life, beginning of 14, 16
life, history of *14–15*
'lizard-footed' dinosaurs see sauropods
'lizard-hipped' dinosaurs see saurischians

lobe-fins 19
loggerhead turtle 77
Lucas, O. W. 13
Lycaenops 23
Lystrosaurus 25, 26

M
magnolia 27, *27*
mammals *10*, 26, 27, 81, 82
Mantell, Gideon 11
Marsh, Othniel Charles *11*, 12, 13
megalosaurs 41, 42, *49*
Megalosaurus 11, *40*, 41, *53*
Melanorosaurus 32
Mesozoic Era 14, *14–15*, 16, 25, *69*, 76, 77, *80*, *83*
microsaurs 21
millipede *21*
Mixosaurus 74
monkey puzzle tree *25*
Morganucodon *25*
mosasaurs 77, 80
mould 9
mudskipper *19*

N – O
North America, fossil discoveries in 12, *12*
nothosaurs *73*, 74, 76
nucleic acid 17
Ordovician Period *14*, 17
ornithischians 30, *31*, *50*, 51, 61
Ornitholestes (Coelurus) 45, 46
Ornithomimus 48, 49
ornithopods 30, *30*, *50*, 51, 54, *59*
Ornithosuchus 24
Ostrom, John *45*
Owen, Richard 11

P
Pachycephalosaurus 54, 56
Pachyrhinosaurus 66
palaeontology 7, 87
palaeopathology 89
Palaeoscincus 64
Palaeozoic Era 14, *14–15*, 16, 17, *80*
Pangaea 25, 26
Paradoxides 16
Parasaurolophus 27, *56*, 58
'parrot reptile' see *Psittacosaurus*
pelycosaurs *22*, 23
Pentaceratops 66
period 14
Permian Period *14–15*, 23
Phlegethontia 21
Phobosuchus 76, 77

photosynthesis 17
phytosaurs 26
placodonts 74, 76
Placodus 73
plants 17, 18, 20, 25, *26*, 27, *80,* 81
plateosaurs *29*
Plateosaurus 25, 29, 30
'plate reptiles' *see* stegosaurs
plesiosaurs 26, *26,* 76, 80
pliosaurs *75,* 76
Plot, Robert 41
Polacanthus 63
Precambrian Era 14
Proganochelys 77
Proterosuchus 28, *28*
Protoceratops 43, 44, 64, *64, 65*
Psittacosaurus 64, *64*
Pteranodon 27, 69, 71, *71*
pterodactyloids 71
Pterodactylus 71
pterosaurs 27, *68,* 69, *69, 70,* 79, 80, 82

Q – R
Quaternary Period *14–15*

Quetzalcoatlus 27, 72
Reptiles, Age of 25, 82
reptilians *10,* 20, *21,* 22, *22,* 23, *25,* 26, *27,* 28, 72, *72–73,* 80, 87
rhamphorhynchoids 69
Rhamphorhynchus 68, 69, *69*
rhipidistians *18,* 19
rhynchosaurs 25

S
saurischians 30, *30*
Saurolophines 58, *58*
Saurolophus 58
sauropods *11, 26,* 29, 30, *32,* 33, *34,* 35, *40,* 51, 79, *85,* 89
Scelidosaurus 61, *62*
sclerotic ring *59*
Scolosaurus 63, 63
sea scorpion *17*
seashells 9
seas, life in ancient 17, *17*
seaweed 17, 18
sedimentary rock 14
Silurian Period *14,* 17, *17*

skeleton 7, *9,* 18, *34, 50–51, 73, 75,* 85, *88*
skull *34, 35, 58, 59, 73, 86,* 87
Sordes pilosus 71
Spinosaurus 41
'spiny reptile' *see Styracosaurus*
sponge *16*
Stegoceras 56
stegosaurs 61, *67*
Stegosaurus 61, *61, 88*
Struthiomimus 82
Styracosaurus 66, *83*
Sydenham Park 12

T
Tanystropheus 72, *73*
Tarbosaurus 13
Teleosaurus 77
Tertiary Period *14–15*
thecodont 28
Thecodontosaurus 30
theropods 30
'thorn reptile' *see Scolosaurus*
Thrinaxodon 25

Ticinosuchus 29, *29*
tooth 11, 13, *41*
Torosaurus 67
Trachodon 13
trees *25,* 27, *27, 83*
Triassic Period *14–15,* 25, 29, 30, 69, 72, 73, 74
Triceratops 67, *67*
trilobite *16*
tuatara 25
turtle 77, *77*
Tylosaurus 27
tyrannosaurs 41, 42, *42–43,* 44, *49,* 79
Tyrannosaurus rex 27, 41, 42, *42–43,* 66, 79

V – W – Y
Velociraptor 43, 44
vertebrates 18, 19, *18–19,* 80
Wealden Lizard *10*
'whale lizard' *see Cetiosaurus*
'winged reptiles' *see* pterosaurs
Yaverlandia 54

Acknowledgements

Jacket front: Picturepoint; Jacket back: United States Dept. of the Interior, National Park Service; Endpaper: Biofotos; page 1: Picturepoint; pages 4–5: Geoscience Features; page 8: United States Dept. of the Interior, National Park Service; page 10: Illustrated London News; page 11: Peabody Museum of Natural History; page 12: United States Dept. of the Interior, National Park Service *top,* Courtesy of the American Museum of Natural History *bottom,* Peabody Museum of Natural History *centre;* page 13: Zophia Kielan-Jaworowska; page 16: Levi-Setti, Enrico Fermi Institute; page 17: Imitor; page 19: Bruce Coleman/Jane Burton; page 20: ZEFA *top,* Pat Morris *bottom left,* Michael Chinery *bottom right;* page 25: G. R. Roberts; page 26: Biofotos; page 27: Michael Chinery; page 28: Bruce Coleman/Jen and Des Bartlett; page 37: ZEFA/P. Fera; page 41: Imitor *right,* Pat Morris *bottom;* page 44: Zophia Kielan-Jaworowska; page 46: Museum fur Naturkunde, Berlin; page 54: Bruce Coleman/Stouffer Productions; page 63: British Museum of Natural History; page 68: Pat Morris; page 74: Imitor: page 75: Imitor; page 77: Peabody Museum of Natural History *top,* ZEFA/W. Braun *bottom;* page 81: ZEFA/R. Halin; page 82: Courtesy of the American Museum of Natural History; page 84: United States Dept. of the Interior, National Park Service; page 85: Zophia Kielan-Jaworowska; page 86: Barry Cox; page 87: Imitor *left,* Zophia Kielan-Jaworowska *right;* page 88 Pat Morris; page 89: Picturepoint.

Picture Research: Jackie Cookson
Jacket and Prelim design: Frank Phillips
Artists: Bernard Robinson, The Tudor Art Agency, Linden Artists, The Garden Studio, Temple Art Agency